MORE STRANGE
BUT TRUE
BASEBALL STORIES

Accounts of 34 amazing, amusing and
offbeat moments in baseball history.

MORE STRANGE
BUT TRUE
BASEBALL STORIES

by Howard Liss

Illustrated with photographs

Random House · New York

For two great nephews
and great baseball fans,
James Flick and David Gudisman.

PHOTOGRAPH CREDITS: Brown Brothers: 21; Culver Pictures: 17, 25, 37, 67, 96, 103, 117; United Press International: endpapers, ii–iii, ix, 8, 53, 66, 73, 79, 108, 113, 135; Wide World Photos: 3, 13, 35, 43, 47, 59, 87, 99, 124, 134, 138. Cover art by Ed Vebell.

Library of Congress Cataloging in Publication Data

Liss, Howard.
    More strange but true baseball stories.
    (Major League Library #16)
    SUMMARY: Recounts thirty-four unusual baseball events including, among others, the man who caught a ball thrown from the top of the Washington Monument.
    1. Baseball stories—Juvenile literature. [1. Baseball—Anecdotes]
I. Title.
GV873.L54   796.357   74–37411
ISBN 0–394–82390–7
ISBN 0–394–92390–1 (lib. bdg.)

Contents

Introduction

More peculiar things have happened in baseball than in any other American sport. Perhaps it is because baseball has been played for more years than any other game. Something unusual seems to be going on all the time, not only in average games, but in crucial games where championships are won and lost and new records are set.

Many of the stories in this book are about incidents that didn't matter very much. They are strange and they are true and they will be told as long as baseball is played, but they didn't affect a game or a season very much. But once in awhile a strange play may affect a championship. One play like that happened in the 1970 World Series.

The Cincinnati Reds were facing the Baltimore Orioles and the game was tied in the sixth inning. The Reds were at bat with two out and men on first and third. The batter was pinch hitter Ty Cline, who chopped a high bouncer out in front of the plate.

Then the confusion started. Baltimore catcher Ellie Hendricks ran out to field the ball. Umpire Ken Burkhardt straddled the third-base line to judge whether the ball would be fair or foul. And the runner at third, Bernie Carbo, came steaming down the line toward home.

All three men reached home at the same time. Hendricks got the ball and turned toward the plate to put the tag on the runner. But as he turned, he knocked the umpire down almost in front of Carbo, who was sliding toward the plate. The umpire was facing center field when the play was made. Hendricks tagged Carbo with his glove hand—while holding the ball with his throwing hand. Carbo, who had to slide around the umpire, missed home plate.

As one writer put it, the umpire missed the catcher, who missed the runner, who missed home plate.

Umpire Burkhardt did get a quick look at the play over his shoulder, and he called the runner out. This

Catcher Ellie Hendricks runs into the umpire while trying to tag Cincinnati's Bernie Carbo.

ended the inning for the Reds and they lost the game 4-3. They also lost the Series.

What would have happened if the run had scored? Nobody will ever know, but everybody will enjoy wondering about it. Soon this story will take its place with the hundreds of other odd happenings that have made baseball so interesting, And years from now, when fans are telling their favorite stories of the game, this story and many others in this book will come up again to be laughed at and wondered about.

MORE STRANGE BUT TRUE BASEBALL STORIES

The Great Catch

Gabby Street never was much of a hitter. His highest season's average was .238 in 34 games. In 1908 and 1909 he was the regular catcher for the Washington Senators. However, he batted a lowly .206 one year and .211 the following season, hardly enough to insure him of a regular job.

But as a catcher Street was outstanding. He could hang onto almost any kind of pitch. One of the pitchers he handled with Washington was the famous fast-baller Walter Johnson. Many catchers

could hardly see Johnson's fastball, let alone catch it.

Street was especially good at catching the towering pop fouls that seemed to go high enough to crack through a cloud. He would throw off his mask, judge the flight of the ball, circle under it and make the catch. Some of his catches were truly spectacular. But none were as famous as the catch he made on August 21, 1908—and he wasn't even in a ballpark at the time.

One of Gabby's most loyal supporters was a Washington newspaperman named Pres Gibson. Gibson declared that anyone who could catch Walter Johnson's pitches could handle any other pitcher in the game. Furthermore, Street could catch pop-ups that nobody else could hold.

One evening in August of 1908, Gibson was arguing with another fan about Gabby Street's fielding ability. "I don't care how high the ball is," Gibson said firmly. "If Gabby can reach the ball, he'll hold on to it."

"How about a foul pop that goes up a hundred feet?" asked the other fan.

"Make that two or three hundred feet and Gabby will still get it," Gibson replied.

"Let's see now," said the fan. "The Washington Monument is more than five hundred feet high. Do you think Street is good enough to catch a ball dropped from the top of the Monument?"

"Sure!" retorted Gibson recklessly.

"Bet you he can't!"

"Bet he can!"

Gibson accepted the bet and the two men laid down their money. On August 21st they brought Street to the Monument and the attempt was made. A large crowd had gathered to watch the strange event.

Gibson himself went to the top of Washington Monument, carrying thirteen baseballs. He was so far above the ground that he could hardly see the catcher. Street stood on the grass below the Monument, nervously pounding his fist into his mitt. This was a tough one. A ball that fell that far would have tremendous speed. If he misjudged it, it would surely fracture his skull! Street himself would never have made such an outlandish bet, but now that it had been made, he couldn't let his friend down. He braced himself for the tosses and looked up toward the top of the Monument.

At first Gibson tried dropping the baseballs

straight down, but the first few hit the side of the column and bounced crazily in all directions. Gibson tried throwing a couple straight out, but then Street couldn't reach them.

Finally, someone in the crowd realized that the wind was playing tricks with the ball. Everybody went around to the other side of the Monument, which was shielded from the wind. Gibson resumed throwing the balls.

Only three times did the ball come close enough so that Street could make a try for the catch. Each time he barely missed as the ball dropped just out of reach. At last Gibson had only one baseball left —number thirteen.

Gibson let the last baseball fly. It was a good toss. Street judged the ball perfectly, camped under it and spread his legs wide. Down plummeted the ball. Street reached out. The ball went straight and true into the mitt and Gabby held on for dear life. A great cheer arose from the crowd. Street had made the catch!

As a ballplayer, Gabby Street was undistinguished (although he did go on to become a successful manager). But he had become a famous man that August day. Years later, when he became a soldier in World War I, total strangers would come over to shake his hand because he had caught a baseball thrown from the top of Washington Monument.

The Perfect Relief Pitcher

Managers today divide their relief pitchers into two categories: the "long" man and the "short" man. The long man will enter a game in the early innings—perhaps the second or third—and may pitch more than half the game. He sometimes even starts a game. The short man is used only for an inning or two late in the game.

Often a relief pitcher comes into the game in a bad situation. There may be men on base and the other team may have scored already. The pressure is on the hurler to keep them from scoring another run. He has to bear down on almost every pitch. The reliefer doesn't usually pitch as long as the starter, so he doesn't have to pace himself. As long as he's pitching, he works at full steam.

One of the longest relief jobs and certainly the greatest was pitched on June 23, 1917, by Ernie Shore of the Boston Red Sox. Boston's starter that day against the Washington Senators was a young pitcher named Babe Ruth. The Babe pitched a bit too carefully to Washington's lead-off batter and walked him.

Ruth never was noted for his even temper. He thought a couple of pitches should have been strikes. When the umpire called "Ball four!", Ruth exploded in anger. He stalked over to the umpire and questioned his eyesight. The umpire replied angrily and Ruth swung at the ump, landing a fist on his neck. The Babe was promptly thrown out of the game.

Ernie Shore was sitting on the bench when Ruth was thrown out. Hurriedly summoned to the mound, he had very little time to warm up. Then he faced the second batter in the Washington line-up.

The baserunner, thinking that Shore would not be concentrating on him, decided to steal second. The plan didn't work: a good throw from the catcher got him out.

Then Ernie Shore hitched up his pants and

began to knock off the Washington hitters. One after the other they fell before his curves and fast-balls.

Shore didn't walk a man. Shore didn't allow a hit. Nobody got on base against him. Ernie Shore hurled a complete perfect game as a relief pitcher!

Actually, Shore was usually a starting pitcher for the Red Sox. But he did come into this game as a reliefer. No pitcher since then has duplicated his feat. Since there was nobody out when he began his relief stint, and Shore was responsible for all 27 outs, he was credited with pitching a perfect game, one of the few in baseball's record book.

Ernie Shore.

The Comeback

Many ballclubs owe their success to a team leader who is able to inspire the rest of the players. Such a leader may be a fiery character or a "holler guy." But sometimes he is a quiet, steady player who sets the example for the others to follow.

The New York Yankees had some great team leaders through the years. In the 1920s it was the flamboyant Babe Ruth who sparked the Yanks to victory. Did the team need a key hit to come from behind and take the ball game? As long as the Babe was in the line-up, the Yankees were never out of a game.

In the 1930s, when Ruth retired, the new Yankee leader was first baseman Lou Gehrig. Lou was a quiet man, not given to outbursts of temper. But he was an amazing performer, especially in the clutch. Gehrig never missed a game and he steadied the club, leading them through the good days and the bad.

When Gehrig was finished, the Yankees turned to their magnificent young center fielder, Joe Di-Maggio.

DiMag could do anything a ballplayer was supposed to do on the field—and he did it better than anyone else. The "Yankee Clipper" was a fantastic fielder, and he had deceptive speed and wonderful judgment. He had the knack of making even the most difficult catch look easy. His throwing arm was powerful and accurate. He ran the bases flawlessly.

Most important, there were few righthanded batters in baseball as good as DiMaggio. His lifetime average was .325, and if his home park had not been Yankee Stadium, it would have been far higher. Joe's "power alley" was left-center field, where the fence was 457 feet from home plate. Many of his long, deep drives were caught near the wall; in any other park they would have been home runs.

At the beginning of the 1949 season Joe was approaching the end of his career. He was out of the line-up with a painful heel injury, and for the first part of the season he had to watch the Yanks from the bench.

DiMaggio's foot had bothered him at the end of the 1948 season, and he had barely hobbled through the schedule. It was thought that rest and treatment during the winter would cure the heel. But early in spring training it became sore and tender again. He couldn't even put his full weight on the hurt foot.

The Yankees managed to stay near the top of the league even without DiMaggio. In fact they were leading the league in the middle of June. New York had other great players who could hit the ball a mile—including "King Kong" Keller, Tommy Henrich and Yogi Berra. But without Big Joe in the line-up, somehow the spark was missing.

Then the Boston Red Sox began to threaten the Yankees' lead. The Sox won ten of eleven games during the last half of June. Then on June 29th they met the Yankees for a three-game series in Boston's Fenway Park. The Red Sox were working on a four-game winning streak, and they had the psychological advantage of playing at home.

Up to that time DiMaggio had not played a single inning of regular season baseball for the Yankees. He had sat on the bench, doing what he could to encourage his teammates. But his bat was silent and his foot was still healing.

The day before the Boston series, DiMaggio asked to play in an exhibition game against the New York Giants. This would be the test of his injured foot. Manager Casey Stengel told Joe to play as long as he liked, and to take himself out of the game the moment he felt a twinge in his sore heel. To everyone's surprise, DiMaggio played the entire nine innings. The pain in his heel had disappeared.

The series with Boston was important. If the Sox kept their hot streak alive and beat the Yankees three straight, they would be only a game and a half behind. The Red Sox had won the pennant the year before, and it was important to the Yanks to keep their lead.

"Casey," said DiMaggio as the first game lineups were being prepared, "I'm ready to play now."

DiMaggio wasted no time getting back in the groove. In the second inning he lashed out a single. Two outs later, teammate Johnny Lindell walked, and Hank Bauer followed with a long home run to give the Yanks three runs. In the third inning Phil Rizzuto walked, and DiMaggio came up again. This time he slammed a home run. The Yanks went on to win, 5-4. Big Joe had driven in the tying and winning runs.

In the second game the aroused Red Sox pounded Yankee pitchers Tommy Byrne and Clar-

Joe DiMaggio connects with the ball during a home run contest a few days before he returned to the line-up.

ence Marshall, piling up a 7-1 lead early in the game. In the fifth inning, Joe came to bat with Rizzuto and Henrich on base. The Yankee Clipper unloaded a shot to left field for a home run, bringing the Yanks to within three runs. When he came up in the eighth, the Yanks had tied the score at 7-7. Joe waited for his pitch and boomed the ball out of the park for the winning run.

Game three was the real decider. The Yankees were clinging to a slim 3-2 lead as they came to bat in the seventh inning. Second baseman Snuffy Stirnweiss singled and so did Tommy Henrich. Up stepped Joe DiMaggio. The count went to 3-and-2; Joe drove the next pitch over the left field screen for a home run! Again, the runs were important, because the Sox got a run later. For the third straight day, Joe's bat had made the difference as the Yanks won 6-3.

What a comeback! DiMaggio had not played in a single regular season game until almost the end of June. Other players would have needed time to get their batting eye back—but not Joe. In his first eleven at-bats he had hit four home runs and a single, driving in nine runs.

It was a magnificent series—and a great year— for New York and Joe DiMaggio. The Yanks went on to win the pennant and the World Series. DiMaggio hit .346 over the rest of the season. He had made one of the great comebacks in baseball history.

The Good Luck Charm

Nearly all old-time ballplayers were superstitious. They believed in jinxes that brought bad luck and in all sorts of lucky charms that brought good fortune. If a player suffering a batting slump found a pin on the sidewalk or in a hotel lobby, he was convinced that the slump would soon end. If he enjoyed a good day at the plate, he would eat the same foods the next day, wear the same clothes, take the same route to the ballpark. He was convinced that if he did everything the same way his luck would continue.

Early in the 1911 season, the New York Giants were playing in St. Louis. A slender young man walked over to the bench before the game and introduced himself as Mr. Charles Victory Faust. Young Faust told manager John McGraw of a strange experience he had. A fortune teller in Kansas City had predicted that if he pitched for the Giants, the team would win the pennant.

McGraw was as superstitious as any player. At the mention of a "fortune teller," he told Faust to grab a glove and pitch in a few. Faust, still wearing his best Sunday suit, obliged. McGraw himself did the catching.

Faust's windup was crazy. His arms waved wildly in circles, going over his head and across his body, so that he looked like a windmill with loose vanes. And when he finally did throw the ball, it had no speed at all.

It didn't matter whether McGraw called for a curve, a change-up or fastball. All of Faust's pitches were delivered the same way and at the same speed. Finally McGraw tossed away the mitt and asked the would-be major leaguer to try his hand at batting.

By that time many of the players had gathered around and decided to have some fun at the expense of the young man. A few of them took positions in the field while Faust selected a bat and went to the plate.

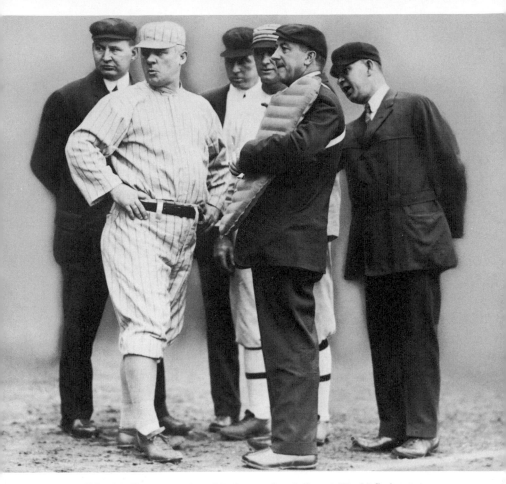

John McGraw consults with the umpires before a World Series game.

Then the batting practice pitcher sent a medium-speed pitch right over the heart of the plate. Faust swung with all his might and tapped a slow roller to the left side of the infield. The shortstop deliberately allowed the ball to slip out of his hands. While he was chasing it, Faust rounded first base and headed for second.

As he slid hard into the bag, the second baseman

let the ball get away—on purpose, of course—and
Faust dug for third, sliding into that base. The
third baseman got into the spirit of the play and he
also committed an error. Faust got to his feet and
dashed for home, sliding across the plate. He never
stopped to think that he was wearing his best suit
of clothes.

When the New York Giants took the train out of
St. Louis, Charles Victory Faust went with them.
McGraw had a hunch that this chap would bring
the team good luck. Faust was given a uniform and
spending money, but no contract. That didn't matter to Faust, who was convinced he was destined to
pitch the Giants to a pennant. Every day he would
warm up as if he expected to pitch. The players
would watch good-naturedly and comment on his
delivery.

As a matter of fact McGraw did allow him to
pitch. The record books show that in 1911 Charles
Faust appeared in two games. By then Faust was a
well-known figure, and many fans wanted to see
him do something on the field. McGraw got permission from the other team, since Faust wasn't
officially on the New York roster.

The first time Faust went to the box, the opposing batters didn't have the heart to score a run on
him. And when the time came for Faust to bat
there were already three out in the inning, but the
good luck charm was permitted to take his swings.

As before, in St. Louis, Faust hit a grounder to the infield and went sliding into all the bases as the infielders kept making "errors," much to the delight of the fans.

Charles Victory Faust's records show that he pitched one inning in each of two games. He allowed one run in the second game. At the plate, he was not credited with any times at bat, yet, somehow, the records show that he scored one run and stole two bases!

And Faust *did* turn out to be a lucky charm, for the Giants won the pennant in 1911. Faust was the New York good luck charm in 1912 and 1913, and each time the New York team won the flag in the National League.

At the end of the 1913 season Faust told McGraw that he wasn't feeling well. There was some talk of sending him away for a vacation so that he might regain his health and be ready to join the Giants the following season.

But Faust was too sick. The Giants played their 1914 schedule without their good luck charm. That year the Boston Braves must have found their own charm. Boston was in last place on July 4th, but after that they drove all the way to first place and won the pennant.

Charles Victory Faust did not live to see his beloved New York Giants win another pennant. The "good luck man" died on June 18, 1915.

Babe Ruth's Curve Ball

When baseball scouts first spotted Babe Ruth, he was playing for St. Mary's Industrial School in Baltimore, Maryland. Some people called it an orphanage, but it was really more of a reform school for the tough kids of the city.

Ruth was a pitcher then, although he could already hit the ball a mile. One day a man named Jack Dunn, who scouted for the Baltimore Orioles, came to the school to look over another St. Mary's pitcher. One of the Catholic Brothers told Dunn

about a good prospect named George Herman
Ruth. Dunn saw Ruth in action and promptly
signed him to an Oriole contract. Soon the Babe
was pitching for the Orioles.

Babe had a lot to learn about pitching. When
one slugger came to bat, the Oriole catcher called
time out and went to the mound for a conference
with Ruth.

"Babe, this guy looks anxious," said the catcher.
"I think he'll swing at almost anything. Throw him

Babe Ruth as a young pitcher for the Boston Red Sox.

a waste pitch first just to see what he'll do." The catcher meant that Ruth should pitch a ball—high and way outside.

Ruth went into his windup and sent a fastball over the plate. The batter hit it over the center fielder's head and circled the bases for a home run.

"Boy, were you ever wrong," Babe told the catcher bitterly.

"Are you crazy?" the catcher retorted. "You crossed me up. I told you to waste one, and you put it right over the plate."

Then Babe understood. "Oh," he said with a sheepish grin, "I thought you wanted a *waist* pitch." And he tapped the middle of his stomach.

Ruth was far from being a steady pitcher. When he sent in his fastball, he often overpowered the hitters. But after a while, the opposing batters began to blast his curve ball. They didn't swing at his fast pitches, but waited until he threw the curve. It almost seemed that they knew when to expect the curve.

The coaches worked with Babe, watching his form, the way he held the ball in his glove, his windup and delivery. They couldn't see how he was "telegraphing" the batters that he was about to throw a curve. Everyone was baffled.

It was an outfielder named Harry Hooper, destined to become an outstanding major leaguer, who finally discovered what Babe was doing wrong. He studied Babe intently. And finally he saw one little thing that kept repeating itself every time Babe delivered the curve ball.

"Watch the kid's face," he said to Jack Dunn.

Dunn watched. "I don't see anything," he said, puzzled.

"His tongue! Look at his tongue!" Hooper pointed impatiently toward the mound. "Every time he's going to throw the curve, he sticks his tongue through the corner of his mouth. *That's* what the other teams saw and we didn't."

Sure enough, as Babe went into his windup to throw the curve, the tip of his tongue popped through the corner of his mouth.

The coaches soon corrected Ruth's mistake, and he became an outstanding American League pitcher. In fact, he might have become one of the greatest pitchers in history. But his teams found that he was even more valuable as a hitter and he was switched to the outfield. When he stood at the plate, ready to hit another long home run, it didn't matter whether he stuck his tongue out or not.

"Let
Me See
the Ball!"

As a pitcher, Al Schacht didn't last very long in the
major leagues. The records show that he pitched
for the Washington Senators from 1919 to 1921,
and in those three years he won 14 and lost 10.
Most of his victories were lucky. But Schacht was
also one of the funniest men in baseball. His antics
and "shows" were hilarious. Major and minor
league teams would hire him to entertain the customers before a game, or during the intermission
between the games of a doubleheader. The fans al-

ways enjoyed his capers, and Schacht had a good time performing.

One of the most amusing incidents involving Schacht happened after his big league career was over. He was pitching for Reading (Pennsylvania) in the 1920s, and part of the time he put on shows for the customers. Once when Reading was scheduled to play Baltimore, Schacht put on a comical display with a fungo bat and a ten-cent baseball. He pretended to play "baseball-golf," socking the

Al Schacht (left) takes a picture of another clown, Washington's Nick Altrock.

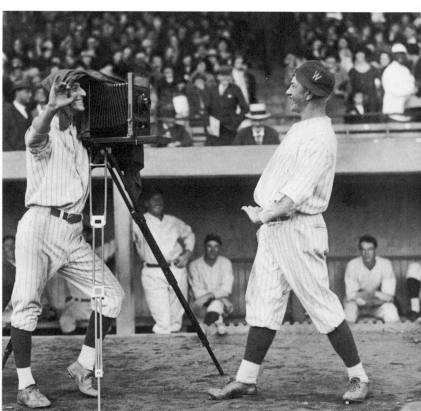

sawdust-filled ball on the fly, then "putting" toward an imaginary hole. When the show was over, Schacht put away the fungo bat, stuffed the ball in his pocket, and ambled out to the bullpen to be ready in case he was needed.

Sure enough, in the ninth inning, Reading's manager called for Schacht to come in and pitch. As he strode toward the pitcher's box, Schacht suddenly realized that the dime baseball was still in his pocket.

Schacht realized that he had an opportunity for some extra fun, and he couldn't resist the temptation. He picked up the regulation baseball, then called his catcher to meet him at the mound for a "conference."

"Look, I've still got this goofy baseball," he said to the catcher, whereupon he stuffed the real baseball into his shirt and put the dime ball into his glove. "From the first pitch on, you get that ball back to me as fast as you can. Don't let the umpire see it!"

The befuddled catcher nodded and returned to his position. He gave the signal, although he had no idea what kind of pitch Schacht would deliver with that sawdust baseball.

The first batter was Joe Boley, who would soon play in the majors for the Philadelphia Athletics. Boley was a powerful hitter, noted for his sizzling line drives. He dug in and glared at Schacht.

The first pitch was right over the plate, chest high. Boley swung with all his might. The ball popped 20 feet into the air and settled comfortably in Schacht's glove. Scratching his head, Boley trudged back to the dugout, wondering what had happened.

Schacht noticed that his dime baseball had been knocked slightly out of shape by Boley's blast. Quickly he squeezed it back into shape and faced the next batter.

Once again he sent a straight, medium-speed pitch right over the plate. Another swing—and again the ball popped into the air right back at Schacht.

By then the ball was a lopsided mess. Desperately Schacht squeezed it until it was approximately round again and faced the last Baltimore batter, pitcher Rube Parnham, who was a pretty good hitter.

Parnham teed off on Schacht's toss and really hit it. The ball popped up, and then began to flutter, dip and sail like a wounded sparrow. Parnham watched in disbelief as the ball plopped into Schacht's glove for the third out. Then with a roar of rage, he demanded that the umpire examine the ball. Before Schacht could get rid of it, the umpire was at his side.

"Let's have the ball," the umpire demanded.

"It's the trick ball," Schacht admitted. But then,

his quick mind racing, the sore-armed pitcher saw a way out of his dilemma.

"Listen, ump," he said. "I got Boley and Stiles out with the real baseball. But then when I saw Parnham coming to bat, I decided to have some fun. You know how he's always talking mean to all the guys. I just wanted to show him up, that's all."

The umpire hesitated for a moment. It was true; Parnham sometimes did get other players angry because he was always "popping off" at them. Schacht, seeing that the umpire might be swayed, pressed his advantage.

"Let Parnham bat all over again," he coaxed. "I'll use the real baseball."

"Okay," agreed the umpire. "But no more tricks!"

Parnham was so angry by then that he couldn't control his swing. Schacht sent a slow curve to the plate. Parnham swung and popped up to the pitcher.

But You were Wrong,Ump!

Ballplayers sometimes say that umpires should have been called "dictators" instead, because whether they are wrong or right, nobody can change their minds.

Players and umpires have always argued about close plays. Was it a ball or a strike? Was the runner safe by half an inch, or out by half an inch? Television's instant replay now makes it easy even for a fan to second-guess an umpire and perhaps prove him wrong. Before the coming of films and television it was almost impossible to prove an umpire's decision one way or another.

One day in 1946 a situation arose in which the umps were proved dead wrong without any replay machines—but it took a full day to get the evidence. The Jersey City Giants were playing the Newark Bears at Newark. Buster Maynard, the Jersey City left fielder, took a healthy swing at the ball and sent it zooming out toward the left-field fence. Maynard was convinced he had slugged a home run. He was heading for third base when suddenly umpires Scotty Robb and Artie Gore signaled him to return to second base. The umpires said they had seen the ball strike the top of the outfield fence and bounce back onto the playing field—making the hit a ground-rule double.

Instantly the Jersey City players went swarming onto the field, protesting that the ball had gone into the stands and bounced back onto the field.

Of course the umpires won the argument. But the following day a Newark newspaper carried a story proving that while umpires have the last word in a dispute, they aren't necessarily right.

A boy who was sitting in the left-field stands had been hit on the head by Maynard's drive. The ball had bounced off the boy's head and back onto the field. He had been sent to a hospital for observation, but he was not seriously injured.

Still, the umpires' decision stood. Buster Maynard was credited with a double, not a homer. Buster Maynard complained that he had been *robb*ed. Umpire Scotty Robb didn't think the joke was funny.

Heads-Up
Baseball

Any list of great second basemen would have to include Eddie Collins. Many stories have been written about his great fielding, his clutch hitting and his classy base running. He broke into the American League in 1907 with the Philadelphia Athletics. In 1915 he was sent to Chicago and starred for the White Sox for twelve years. In 1927 he returned to the Athletics and played out his career as part-time infielder and pinch hitter. His lifetime batting average was .333 and he stole 743 bases, the second-best record in history.

But no record book can show a man's true value to a team. For Collins was more than a great player with his hands and his bat. There was no one in the game smarter or quicker to see the possibilities of an ordinary play. Nothing escaped his hawk eyes. Furthermore, he knew the rule book by heart.

After he quit playing at the age of 44, Collins stayed on with the Athletics. He wasn't just a coach. Collins was appointed captain of the team, even though he no longer took the field with the other players. And once, captain Eddie Collins almost saved a World Series game for the Athletics when it seemed to be all over.

When Philadelphia came to bat in the ninth inning of the second game of the 1931 World Series, the St. Louis Cardinals were leading 2-0. The St. Louis pitcher, Bill Hallahan, had allowed the Athletics just three hits.

The first batter was slugger Jimmy Foxx. Hallahan was a little too careful with Foxx and walked him. The next batter, Bing Miller, flied out. Then Jimmy Dykes walked and Dib Williams struck out. With two on and two out, Jim Moore walked to the plate. Hallahan put over two quick strikes. And then things began to happen.

As Hallahan made his next delivery, Jimmy Foxx suddenly broke for third base. Hallahan's pitch was a low curve, bouncing into the dirt. But Moore swung and missed for strike three.

Card Catcher Jimmy Wilson made a fine pickup of the pitch. Seeing Foxx streaking for third, Wilson instinctively fired the ball toward third. But the throw was hurried and off target. Fans heading for the exits stopped, puzzled. What was going on?

Foxx was standing on third, not knowing what to do next. Dykes was on first, scratching his head. The batter was walking toward the dugout, convinced he had struck out.

But Eddie Collins began to shout orders for Foxx to stay on third, for Dykes to run to second, and for Moore to run to first. Bewildered, the Athletics' players obeyed. Then Collins raced to the umpire for his "appeal play."

He pointed out that the ball had bounced in the dirt after the swing. According to the rule then in force, the catcher either had to tag the runner or throw to first in order to retire him. Otherwise, the strikeout didn't count and the runner was safe if he could beat the throw to first base.

Umpire Dick Nallin consulted the rule book and admitted that Collins was right. The game wasn't over: Moore went to first and the bases were loaded with the dangerous Max Bishop coming to the plate. A long single would tie the game and a long extra-base hit would win it for the Athletics.

Unfortunately for Philadelphia, Hallahan bore down and put Bishop out to end the game. But it wasn't Eddie Collins' fault. He had given them a life when the game appeared to be over. Nobody else noticed that the pitch had bounced in the dirt, or if they did, nobody thought of the proper rule. Eddie Collins did.

The record book shows that Eddie Collins was a remarkable second baseman and batter. It doesn't show that he was one of the smartest players as well.

Eddie Collins (left) confers with manager Connie Mack during the 1931 season.

The Record Year for "Old Hoss"

Baseball was a different game in the 1880s. Many of the teams in the major leagues then are unfamiliar to modern fans. Providence, Rhode Island, was one of the teams in the National League. Other teams such as Louisville, Hartford and Indianapolis had entered the league for a few years and dropped out again.

The teams kept changing—and so did the rules. For example, at one time a pitch could bounce on the way to the plate and still be called a strike if it

"Old Hoss" Radbourne.

passed through the strike zone. Pitchers stood 50 feet from the plate instead of the present 60 feet, 6 inches. It took six "balls" or more to walk a batter. Until 1884 pitchers could throw underhand if they desired. The batter could call for a low pitch or a high one. But during the early 1880s, he was out if he hit a foul that was caught on the first bounce! Bats were peculiar too. The rules permitted one side of a bat to be as flat as a paddle.

Still, most of the basic rules of the game were the same and baseball had its stars and great teams just as it has today. One of the pitchers of the 1880s, Charles G. "Old Hoss" Radbourne, would be considered a star in any era. In 1884 he rose to heights which no other pitcher has ever reached.

Old Hoss broke in with Providence in 1881. In practically no time he became one of the pitching greats. In 1882 he won 33 games for Providence,

and the following year he won no less than 48!
Radbourne wasn't a big man, but he had good stuff
on the ball and was hard to hit.

In those days team rosters were very small. A
club couldn't afford special relief pitchers, spare
fielders, a bench full of pinch hitters. In addition,
the rules said that a team couldn't substitute for a
player unless he was injured or the other team gave
its permission. Nearly all players had to play more
than one position. Old Hoss usually played the outfield when he wasn't pitching. He wasn't a bad hitter either. In 1883 he batted .283, but that was ad-
mittedly an exceptional year.

Pitching was Old Hoss's strong point. He proved
that in 1882 and 1883. Radbourne was the best
pitcher in Providence and probably the best in the
league. But in 1884 a flashy new youngster named
Charlie Sweeney, began to challenge Radbourne.
Sweeney was only 22 years old and it seemed that
he might take away Radbourne's position as top
pitcher for Providence.

For the first part of the season, Sweeney matched
Old Hoss pitch for pitch. In fact sometimes his performance was better than Radbourne's. Early in
the year Sweeney pitched a one-hitter against the
Giants. Radbourne, trying to keep pace with
Sweeney, pitched a one-hitter the next day, but he
walked two men while Sweeney didn't walk anybody.

However, as the season wore on, Sweeney couldn't keep up the blistering pace. One day, when he was being hit hard by an opposing team, Providence manager Frank Bancroft ordered Sweeney to switch positions with Radbourne in right field.

"I will not!" roared the temperamental pitcher.

"I say you will!" said Bancroft forcefully. "Radbourne's pitching and you're not!"

Sweeney didn't switch. He walked off the mound and off the Providence team. Later he joined St. Louis in the rival Union League.

Radbourne was left alone as Providence's only good pitcher. Unlike modern pitchers, Old Hoss had to pitch twice or three times a week—or even more often.

But Old Hoss was equal to the occasion. He never seemed to tire that year. Early in August of 1884, he performed a feat which would be completely unbelievable, except that the record books show it to be true.

On Wednesday, August 7th, he pitched against New York and won 4-2. On Friday he pitched an eleven inning, 1-0 victory over Boston, allowing only two hits. Radbourne rested one day, then defeated Boston again 3-1. The following day he was back in action, knocking off Boston again 4-0.

By then Old Hoss thought he deserved a rest. So did the Boston fans, who were sick and tired of losing to Radbourne. But then a friend of Radbourne's came to him with a sad story. The friend had bet $6,000 on Providence and was afraid he would lose the money unless Radbourne pitched. Old Hoss agreed to pitch the game—his third in a row and his fifth in seven days.

"Guess I might just as well," he said. "I pitched 'em all so far, might as well do the job right."

The rubber-armed pitcher took the mound and hurled a 1-0 shutout! He had won five games in a single week, pitched three shutouts and allowed only three runs.

Providence won the National League pennant that year, claiming 84 victories out of 112 games. Radbourne started 73 games—two out of every three that Providence played—and completed 73 games. During one period he won 26 out of 27 games. He pitched 678⅔ innings and struck out 441 batters. His earned run average was 1.38. That year Old Hoss won *sixty* games while losing only twelve.

No other pitcher in baseball history has come even close to such a record, and it is safe to say no pitcher in the future will either.

The
One-Pitch
Victory

As a rule, relief pitchers work hard for their victories. They enter a game when the other team has rallied. Quite often there are men on base. The reliefer must get the ball over the plate, or risk walking a batter. At the same time, if the pitch is too good, the hitter might bang out a base hit and more runs will score.

Even if the relief pitcher does his job, he often gets little credit. He can pitch nearly half-a-game, and yet the starting pitcher will get credit for the win if he was ahead when he was taken out. So relief pitching is often hard work for little credit.

Sometimes, though, a relief pitcher has to do very little work at all. On May 5, 1946, the Pittsburgh Pirates and the Brooklyn Dodgers played a Sunday doubleheader, and the relief pitchers on both teams saw plenty of action. The first game went eleven innings before the Pirates won it, 5-4. During the game the Pirates' reliefer Elwin "Preacher" Roe was called in to pitch to one Dodger batter, and he managed to retire him.

That first game had been a long one, and both managers were worried. They weren't sure that they would be able to play an entire second game. For in Pittsburgh, there was a Sunday curfew law. No inning could start after a certain time, and if the game had not gone five innings or if the score was tied, it would have to be replayed at a later date.

The Pirates jumped out to a 3-0 lead, and by the time the sixth inning rolled around, it appeared that they had enough runs to win the game. Curfew time was approaching. If the Pirates could retire the Dodgers without too much damage, they could stall in their half of the inning just long enough to force the umpires to call the game.

But the Dodgers were not to be denied. In their half of the sixth, they caught fire and soon tied the score, 3-3. Brooklyn had a runner on third base

Preacher Roe, who beat the Dodgers with one pitch, later became a Dodger star.

named Bob Ramazzotti. There were two out. Pittsburgh pitcher Nick Strincevich was in real trouble.

For the second time that day, the Pirates sent for reliefer Preacher Roe. He took his warm-up pitches, then peered in to get the sign from catcher Bill Salkeld. The Dodgers were in a desperate situation. It was close to curfew time, and they would probably not get another turn at bat. They might try something daring to get the runner home.

Salkeld had a hunch that the runner might try to steal home, or that the batter might try to lay down a bunt on a "suicide squeeze play." Salkeld called for a pitch-out. Sure enough, as Roe went into his windup and delivered the ball, Ramazzotti broke from third. The ball arrived before the runner did, and Salkeld tagged him out on a close play. The Dodgers were out and the game was tied 3-3.

In the bottom of the sixth inning, Pittsburgh rallied for a run. When the last Pirate batter went out to end the inning, the umpire signaled that the game was over. The Pirates had won.

Preacher Roe had delivered one pitch to the plate. It wasn't even a strike. But he was the pitcher of record when the Pirates scored the winning run, and Roe became the official winning pitcher after throwing one pitch.

Yet even Roe had been outdone many years earlier by Nick Altrock. Altrock, a hard-throwing lefthander, was brought in from the bullpen to try to snuff out a ninth-inning rally. The opposing team had tied the score. There were two out, a man on first, and a dangerous batter coming to the plate.

Altrock realized that this was a "steal situation." If the runner on first could steal second, he would be in position to score the lead run on an ordinary outfield single.

Altrock went into his stretch, watching the runner out of the corner of his eye. Then, suddenly, he snapped a hard throw to the first baseman, who caught the runner trying to slide back to the bag. The side was out.

In the bottom of the ninth inning Altrock's team managed to score the winning run, and he received credit for the victory. He had not thrown a single pitch to the batter. He had secured the final out by catching a runner off base.

Therefore, Nick Altrock holds the record. He won a ball game without making even one official pitch!

The Courage of a .400 Hitter

Every great hitter cherishes the dream that some season he will put his skill and his luck together and reach the magic .400 batting average. But it is a dream that very few players realize. In order to attain the .400 mark, a batter must get two base hits in every five at-bats.

The last man to approach the magic .400 batting average was Ted Williams, one of the greatest hitters in the history of baseball. For most of 1941, Ted was up around the .400 mark. Indeed, at one point during the season his average soared to .424.

As the season neared its end, Williams kept up his blistering pace. The Red Sox were scheduled to finish out the year with a three-game series, September 27th and 28th, against the Philadelphia Athletics. Before the series began, manager Joe Cronin drew Williams aside.

"Ted," Cronin said earnestly, "you're hitting .401. If I keep you on the bench, you're sure to end the season over the .400 mark. Nobody will think any less of you. Shall I leave your name out of the line-up?"

"No," snapped Williams. "Thanks for the offer, Joe. But if I hit .400, it's going to be for the whole season."

On September 27th, Williams could manage only one hit in four at-bats. His average dropped to .3995—just below .400. It seemed that his golden opportunity had slipped away.

The last day of the season, Williams was back in the line-up for the first game of a doubleheader. He was more determined than ever. Facing him his first time up was rookie pitcher Dick Fowler. Williams waited for his pitch, then swung smartly. The ball went through the infield for a base hit. Williams was again above .400. The second time Williams faced Fowler, a fastball came toward the plate. Ted took a full swing and connected right on

Ted Williams takes a practice swing during the 1941 season.

the nose. The ball went over the fence for a home run!

Later in the game, lefthander Porter Vaughan came in to pitch to Williams. Ted cracked the ball for another base hit!

"Ted, you're hitting .403," Cronin reminded his star slugger. "Would you like to call it a day?"

"Nope! I'm playing it all the way, Joe," Ted replied.

Williams helped himself to a fourth hit before the game was over. There was a big grin on his face as he trotted to the clubhouse for the short rest between games.

"I guess you've had enough for today," Cronin said happily. But Williams shook his head.

"I'm going all the way to the end, Joe."

In that second game, Ted had two more hits. And he finished the season with a .406 average!

Some of the greatest sluggers in baseball never hit .400. Babe Ruth failed, so did Lou Gehrig, Joe DiMaggio, Mickey Mantle, Willie Mays and Hank Aaron. Williams knew that by sitting out the last games of the season he could be sure of gaining lasting fame. But in a great display of courage he refused to sit on the bench. Every time at bat was a risk to his magic .400 mark, but he met the challenge and actually *increased* his average. Thirty years later, not a single major leaguer had matched Williams' feat.

The Cost of a Bonehead Play

There is an "inside" saying in baseball: "More games are lost by errors of *omission* than by errors of *commission*." In other words, it isn't what a player does that might lose a ballgame; it's what he doesn't do!

Many a game has been lost because of carelessness. For example, a base runner may miss a base and be called out. Or a runner on third, ready to score on a fly ball, leaves the base before the catch is made. Once again, if a fielder notices, he can call for the ball and step on third for an automatic out.

Some careless mistakes cost a team a run or a game, but the most famous of all—called Merkle's boner—cost the New York Giants a pennant. The culprit, a young man named Fred Merkle, was only 20 years old and was a utility infielder-outfielder for the Giants. The year was 1908.

To understand what happened, we must return to a game played almost three weeks previous to Merkle's boner, on September 4, 1908. The Cubs, who were fighting the Giants for the pennant, were playing in Pittsburgh. It was the bottom of the ninth inning, score tied, Pirates at bat. Pittsburgh's Warren Gill was on first, Fred Clarke was the runner on third, and the great shortstop Honus Wagner was the hitter.

Wagner lined the ball over the infield for a clean hit. Clarke trotted in from third with the winning run. But Gill, seeing that Clarke had scored, pulled up short of second base and returned to the dugout.

Cub second baseman Johnny Evers saw Gill's error and he called for the ball. He caught it, stepped on second, then turned to umpire Hank O'Day.

"The runner didn't touch second! I claim a force play!" he shouted to O'Day.

The umpire considered for a moment, then shook his head. "Sorry," he said to Evers, "I didn't see it so I can't call it." And no amount of complaining by Evers could change his decision. The game went into the books as a Pirate victory. But Evers was right: if the umpire had been watching, Warren Gill would have been out and the run would not have counted.

The tight pennant race went right down to the wire. On September 22nd, Chicago came to New York for a three-game series with the league-leading Giants. The first two games were hotly contested, and when the dust had settled, Chicago had won them both by scores of 4-3 and 3-1. New York still had a slender lead, but another Cub victory would bring them too close for comfort. The Giants had lost their last four games.

Manager John McGraw was desperate. To salvage at least one victory from the series, he called on his ace, Christy Mathewson. As usual, Matty came through with a masterful performance. He allowed the Cubs only one run. But the Giants weren't hitting either, and as they came up for their at-bats in the bottom of the ninth, the score was tied, 1-1.

Then the determined Giants put on a rally. With two men out the New Yorkers were in position to win. Moose McCormick was on third, Fred Merkle was on first, and Al Bridwell came to the plate.

As the home town crowd roared with delight, Bridwell cracked a clean hit to center. McCormick trotted in with what appeared to be the winning run.

But here history repeated itself! Fred Merkle did the same thing Warren Gill had done eighteen days earlier. He stopped short of second base and ran off the field. This time Frank Chance, Chicago's first baseman, noticed that Merkle had not touched second and screamed for the ball. It was relayed to him and he ran toward second. If he could touch the bag, Merkle would be out, the run would not count and the game would go into extra innings.

But one of the Giant pitchers, Iron Man McGinnity, realized what was happening. As the crowd poured onto the field celebrating the "victory," McGinnity dashed out of the dugout and chased Frank Chance up the baseline. He managed to catch the Cub infielder and grabbed for the ball. There was a wild scramble amid the milling spectators. McGinnity finally got the ball away from Chance and flung it into the crowd.

Chance got to his feet and saw umpire Hank O'Day nearby—the same umpire who had refused to call the play against the Pirates. Once more the appeal was made. Chance claimed a force play at second on the grounds that McGinnity had illegally interfered while the ball was still in play.

Fred Merkle.

Hank O'Day—and his fellow umpire, Robert Emslie—admitted that neither of them had seen the actual play. However, O'Day ruled Merkle was out! O'Day explained that it was because a force play *might* have been made. Also, there had been interference by the crowd and by McGinnity.

In spite of the Giants' angry appeals, the decision stood. The game was declared a tie, and would be replayed at the end of the season if it had a bearing on the final outcome of the pennant race.

Meanwhile, there was one more game left in the Cubs-Giants series. McGraw sent George "Hooks" Wiltse to the mound. For six innings Wiltse held the Cubs in check while New York gained a five-run lead. In the seventh, Chicago rallied and scored four times. With one out, John McGraw went to the bull pen for a pitcher he knew would put out the fire. That pitcher was Christy Mathewson! Taking the mound in relief, even though he had pitched nine tough innings the day before, Matty stopped the Cubs cold. In two and two-thirds innings, the New York star allowed only one hit and struck out three batters. The Giants won, 5-4.

In the closing week of the season the Giants couldn't hold on to their lead, however, and when the regular schedule was finished, they were tied with the Cubs. The Merkle game would have to be replayed. The Cubs won the replay and the pennant.

Fred Merkle went on to become a good first baseman and a fair hitter, playing 14 more years in the majors. But he never did anything that made him as famous as what he neglected to do that September afternoon in 1908. He had only forgotten to touch second base, but his error of omission had cost the Giants the pennant. For years afterward, whenever a ballplayer made a costly mistake, his teammates would say he committed a Merkle.

There is an odd footnote to the Merkle story. Christy Mathewson, who pitched the famous tie game, went on to win 373 games according to most record books. Years after Matty retired, Grover Cleveland Alexander also won his 373rd game, to tie Mathewson.

If Fred Merkle had not failed to touch second base eight years earlier, Christy Mathewson would have been credited with one more victory, giving him a total of 374, and he would have been the winningest pitcher in National League history.

The Pitchers' Series

In a World Series, a great deal depends on the pitchers. In a majority of the games the score is close. But the hitters on most World Series teams are good, so not many games end in shutouts. As a rule there are never more than one or two per World Series. But the 1905 clash between the New York Giants and the Philadelphia Athletics was quite different.

Both teams were loaded with winning pitchers. Connie Mack's Athletics had a 26-game winner in

Eddie Plank, and Rube Waddell had won 24. Andy Coakley had earned 20 victories, while "Chief" Bender won 16 that season. John McGraw's Giants boasted the best pitcher in the major leagues in Christy Mathewson, who had won the staggering total of 32 games. "Iron Man" McGinnity had rung up 21 wins.

Even before the Series began, the Athletics received a terrific blow to their hopes. In the last weeks of the season, their brilliant pitcher Rube Waddell was injured. Fans were disappointed that they wouldn't see Rube face Christy Mathewson. But still they were predicting a great pitchers' Series.

Almost 18,000 fans jammed the Philadelphia ballpark to witness the first game, a duel between Christy Mathewson and Eddie Plank. People were standing on the field behind the foul lines, held back by special policemen, and more fans were sitting atop the fences. They saw quite a pitching battle between these two masterful hurlers.

Midway in the game the Giants managed to get on the scoreboard. Mathewson singled, but was forced at second by Bresnahan. Then Bresnahan promptly stole second to get into scoring position and scored on a double. A walk and another two-bagger resulted in another big run. Later the Giants added an insurance run.

Meanwhile, the great "Matty" kept mowing

58

down the opposing batters. He gave up only four hits as the Giants won 3-0.

The Athletics tied the Series in game two. Chief Bender and Iron Man McGinnity battled each other inning after inning. This time Bender allowed only four hits as Connie Mack's men made off with a 3-0 victory. The Athletics runs all came after Giant errors, so McGinnity went down to defeat without allowing a single earned run.

The next day it rained, giving Mathewson an extra day's rest. He started again in the third game, facing Philadelphia's Andy Coakley. Once again the Giants' southpaw came out on top. His fastball crackled through the autumn air, and his famous "fadeaway" pitch had the Philadelphia batters connecting only with the air. Once more he gave up only four hits. Coakley's teammates committed five errors, and the New York batters made some timely hits. Final score was 9-0, Giants. Only two of the Giants' nine runs were earned.

The fourth game was a thriller. Iron Man McGinnity dueled Eddie Plank, and it was only through an error that either team scored. An error by the A's second sacker Monte Cross allowed a Giant batter to reach first safely. He went to second on an infield out and scored when a bouncing

Christy Mathewson warms up before a game.

ball took a bad hop and caromed off the third base-
man's glove. That was all the scoring in the game.
The Giants won 1-0 on another unearned run and
McGinnity scored the fourth shutout of the Series.

Desperately, Connie Mack sent in Chief Bender
to pitch the fifth game, for Bender was the only
Philadelphia pitcher who had won a game.
McGraw countered with his ace, Christy Mathewson. Matty hurled a brilliant six-hit shutout. The
Giants took the game and the series with a 2-0 victory.

It had truly been a pitchers' series. *Every game
had ended in a shutout!* Matty had three and
McGinnity and the A's Chief Bender each had one.
Even more amazing, the Giant hurlers had not allowed Philadelphia a single earned run! If the fielders had not made errors, the A's might have been
shut out every time. As for the Philadelphia stars,
they had given up only seven earned runs themselves. In almost any other World Series, their performance would have won for sure.

The disappointed fans who had wanted to see
Rube Waddell were amazed at the shutout Series.
But they insisted that if Rube had been in there, he
would have pitched another shutout or two for
himself.

A Quick
Home Run

Some fans complain that modern baseball is too slow. And perhaps in some ways they are right. Today the average game takes approximately two hours and fifteen minutes to play, from the opening pitch to the final out. Years ago a nine-inning contest lasted less than an hour and a half.

Yet, even at the turn of the century, a few fans thought games lasted too long. High baseball officials seemed to agree. By 1911 the American League had a new rule designed to speed up a ball game. Ban Johnson, president of the league, decreed that pitchers must not take warm-up pitches before the start of an inning.

Few hurlers obeyed the rule. As their teammates were taking the field after their turn at bat, the pitchers would generally manage to toss a few to the catcher. On one occasion, a pitcher tried to take his warm-up pitches and it cost him a run.

It happened in 1911 when Boston was playing the Philadelphia Athletics. Red Sox hurler Ed Karger walked out to the mound, picked up the ball, and began to toss a few to his catcher, Les Nunamaker. The day was particularly warm and humid, so the Red Sox fielders took their time moving back to their positions.

"Stuffy" McInnis, the Philadelphia first baseman, was due at the plate. He watched casually as Karger tossed a pitch to his catcher, and then stepped easily into the batter's box. It didn't look as if he meant to do anything but stand there while Karger finished warming up.

Suddenly, as Karger delivered another pitch, McInnis stepped in and whaled it far into the outfield. The fielders had no chance to catch up with the ball, and McInnis circled the bases for a home run.

The Red Sox protested, but to no avail. For Karger was not supposed to take warm-up pitches. Since he had broken the rule, his pitches had to be counted balls or strikes. McInnis had a perfect right to hit any pitch delivered by an opposing hurler. That was umpire Egan's ruling.

The rule about no warm-up pitches proved very unpopular, and soon it was removed. And fans still complain that baseball is a slow game.

Extra Innings

Very few modern pitchers last through an entire nine-inning game. Many reasons are given. Some say the pitchers don't know how to pace themselves. They throw the ball too hard and too quickly after receiving the return throw from the catcher. Others maintain that the new "lively" ball does the damage. Pitchers are forced to throw as hard as possible, they say, because the ball makes it easier for batters to hit home runs.

Old-timers won't accept these excuses. And they

point to the Brooklyn pitching staff of 1920 as proof that the great hurlers of yesterday were better and stronger pitchers. On May 1st, 2nd and 3rd of that year, Brooklyn and its pitchers endured the longest three days of baseball in history.

On the afternoon of May 1st, Boston's Joe Oeschger and Brooklyn's Leon Cadore met in a pitching duel. The Dodgers managed to score a run in the fifth inning, the Braves eked out a run an inning or two later. Then the two teams settled down to a grim, scoreless battle. Inning after inning went by, and neither side was able to dent the plate again.

Great fielding plays shut off scores for both teams. In the ninth Boston had the bases loaded with only one out. Brooklyn's infielder, Ivy Olson, picked up a hot grounder, tagged the runner coming into second base, then threw to first for the double play.

The innings sped by until the 17th. This time Boston's infield pulled off a wild double play. The Dodgers had the bags full with one out. A comeback grounder was hit to the pitcher, who threw home to force the runner from third base. However, catcher Hank Gowdy's throw to first went wild. Ed Konetchy, the runner who started from second, tried to score on the bad throw, but the ball was recovered and fired to Gowdy, who dove into Konetchy's spikes and made the tag. Gowdy had

Hank Gowdy, the Braves' catcher.

made both put-outs and committed an error in between.

Still the innings rolled on. The old National League record of 22 innings was passed. Then the major league record of 24 innings was also broken.

Finally darkness closed in. Neither players nor umpires could see the ball. The game was called after 26 innings; the 1-1 tie would have to be replayed at a later date.

Wearily the Dodgers took a train home to play against the Philadelphia Phillies the next day. Brooklyn's great spitball pitcher, Burleigh Grimes, engaged Philadelphia's George Smith, and the teams battled tooth and nail. The Dodgers were losing 3-2 when Brooklyn came to bat in the ninth.

Outfielder Zack Wheat came to the rescue. He slammed a home run—and sent the game into extra innings.

The 10th, 11th and 12th went by, scoreless. Philadelphia broke the deadlock in the 13th, when a sacrifice fly with the bases loaded scored a run. That was how the game ended. The Phillies won, 4-3.

The Dodger schedule called for them to go back to Boston. So after their loss to the Phillies, they returned to play another game against the Braves. This time Sherrod Smith took the mound for Brooklyn, while Dana Fillingim drew the assignment for Boston. It seemed that the two teams were right back where they had left off two days ago.

Once more Brooklyn scored first, and then Boston tied it up. The 1-1 deadlock went into extra in-

Burleigh Grimes pitched 13 innings against the Phillies and lost.

nings. The Dodgers were exhausted from two days of extra innings and the Braves weren't fresh either. This time it took 19 innings to decide the outcome. The Braves scored in the 19th and won 2-1.

For the Dodgers, it had been a frustrating, heartbreaking three days of baseball. They had played a total of *58 innings,* equal to three doubleheaders plus four innings thrown in for good measure. All they had to show for it was two losses and one tie game. But this hard-luck team—and their opponents—set some amazing records.

Most amazing of all were the records of the pitchers. All the starting pitchers, for Brooklyn, Philadelphia and Boston, went the route. No relief pitchers were brought in by either side!

Leon Cadore, who allowed only one run to score in 26 innings, never was the same again. His arm was so sore he couldn't lift it for days. Right after the game was over, he went to bed and slept for a day and a half!

Seven weeks later, Boston and Brooklyn replayed their tie game. Boston won.

The ending to the Dodgers' story is partly happy and partly sad. They recovered their luck to win the National League pennant by seven games. In the World Series, they lost to Cleveland five games to two. Sore-armed Leon Cadore started one of the World Series games, but he was knocked out of the box after giving up two runs in the first inning.

The Strangest Double Play

On occasion, things happen in the minor leagues which would probably never take place in the majors. Perhaps it's because big leaguers are more familiar with baseball's rules, or maybe playing experience has something to do with it. At any rate, one game between Williamsport (Pennsylvania) and Elmira (New York) produced one of the strangest rulings any umpire was ever called upon to make.

Elmira had the bases loaded with only one out. The next hitter smacked a hard grounder along the third base line. Williamsport's third sacker scooped up the ball and stepped on the base, forcing out the runner coming from second base. Then he fired toward first, hoping to complete the double play.

Unfortunately, the throw went wild. The Elmira base runners kept going—including the runner who had been forced out at third. He rounded third and headed for home plate. The first baseman caught up with the ball, wheeled and pegged to the catcher, who put the tag on the runner who had already been forced out.

It looked as if the inning had ended with a double play: the force-out and the tagged runner. But then it was discovered that the *same runner* had been called out twice!

Elmira protested to the umpire. Since a runner could be called out only once in any inning, Elmira should still be at bat.

The umpire didn't see it that way. He called the runner out for interference. Elmira protested that a player who had been called out once couldn't be called out again. The umpire stuck to his guns. The inning was over and Williamsport came to bat.

So far as is known, that particular play has only happened once. How would *you* have called it if you were the umpire?

Pitch
Slower,
Win
Faster

Few baseball managers could judge baseball talent
better than Leo Durocher. He rarely made mistakes. But one of his mistakes was pretty important—he misjudged the talent of Sandy Koufax.

The first time Durocher saw Koufax throw was
in June, 1954. Durocher was manager of the New
York Giants and Sandy had come for a tryout. A
utility infielder named Bobby Hofman put on a
chest protector and a mitt to catch for Koufax.
Pitching coach Frank Shellenback watched. Du-

rocher happened to be passing by and stopped to take a look. What he saw made the manager shudder.

Every pitch by Koufax was a fastball, a blur of white that was so fast it was hard to follow. But almost every pitch was wild, bouncing into the dirt, sizzling to the right or left of the plate, or going over Hofman's head. Sure, he was fast, but he had absolutely no control. A batter would just wait for a base on balls, because Koufax threw as though he had never heard of the strike zone. The Giants passed him up.

In September of 1954 Sandy had a tryout with the Brooklyn Dodgers. He was supposed to pitch batting practice, but it had rained that day. Instead, he pitched a few to substitute catcher Rube Walker. Looking on were manager Walter Alston, chief scout Al Campanis, and Dodger executive Fresco Thompson.

Sandy was still as fast and as wild as ever. But Campanis was impressed. "If only that boy could learn control," the scout thought to himself, "he'd be unbeatable."

The Dodgers had had bad luck with other fast-ballers in the past. One, a strong righthander named Rex Barney, had even pitched a no-hitter, but he never developed the control a major league pitcher needs.

Still, the Dodgers offered Koufax a contract with

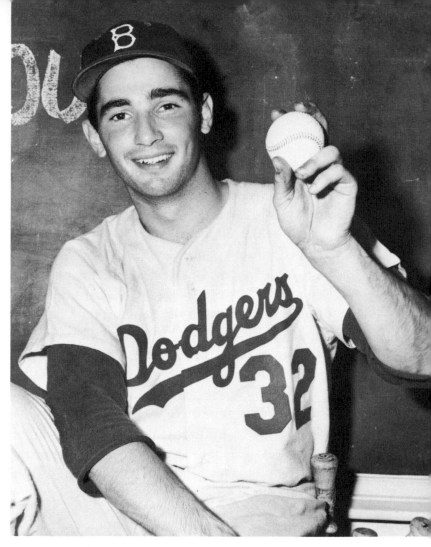

Young Sandy Koufax beams after striking out 14 men in 1955. Six years later he learned the secret of stardom.

a $20,000 bonus. The Braves, who had also been interested in Sandy, had offered more money, but Koufax elected to go with the Dodgers.

The pitching coaches began to work with Koufax

the following spring, but not much came of their efforts. Sandy was too eager to make good, and as a result he developed a sore arm. His arm got better, but his wildness didn't.

Slowly, Sandy was worked into a few ball games. Manager Walt Alston never knew from one day to the next whether Koufax could locate the strike zone or not. In one game he might do well and get the ball over. The next time he would walk everybody who came to the plate. In one game against the Pirates, Sandy lasted $4\frac{2}{3}$ innings. In that short time he made over 100 pitches, usually enough for a whole game. He struck out four batters, but he walked eight men and allowed three hits. The Pirates scored only one run, but Koufax' pitching was the kind that gives managers gray hair.

But the Dodgers refused to give up on Koufax. In his first six years he lost more games than he won. It seemed that wildness would keep him from ever being a big winner.

Then in the spring of 1961, Sandy had a conversation with the Dodgers' second-string catcher, Norm Sherry.

"Sandy, why don't you use a curve ball more often?" asked the catcher.

"Because a fastball is my best pitch," replied Sandy.

"That's one of your troubles," said Sherry. "The hitters know that when you're behind, you're going to come in with your fastball. They're waiting for it."

"I can't control my curve," said Koufax sadly.

"You can't control your fastball either," countered Sherry. "Have you ever thought of throwing your fastball a little slower? Even if you took something off it, you'd still be as fast as anybody in the majors."

And that was the beginning of the great change in Sandy Koufax. Success didn't happen overnight. It took time, because Sandy Koufax changed his whole pitching style. He shortened his stride in his pitching motion, learned to throw the curve ball more often, to hide his pitches from the batters and opposing coaches. His fastball still was a blur to most batters. They refused to believe that he was throwing "softer."

The final result? That year, 1961, Sandy won 18 games. He struck out 269 batters, breaking Christy Mathewson's National League record. But most exciting of all, he walked only 96 batters in 256 innings. The following year he won only 14 games because of a circulation problem in his fingers.

In the next four years he won 25, 19, 26 and 27 games. He hurled four no-hitters, including one perfect game. In addition, he broke nearly every strikeout record in the books. It seems strange, but Sandy Koufax became a winning pitcher when he learned to throw his fastball a little bit slower.

The Asterisk Record

This is an asterisk: *.

In books of records and statistics, including baseball record books, asterisks are used to indicate that some special information about the record is shown at the bottom of the page.

Baseball fans first began paying attention to asterisks at the end of the 1961 season. Roger Maris was trying to break Babe Ruth's record of 60 home runs in a season. Babe had hit his 60 homers in 1927, when each major league team played 154 games a year. But in 1961, Maris' team was playing 162 games. This presented a problem for the record-keepers. If Maris hit his 60th homer after more than 154 games, did he still tie Ruth's record?

After 154 games Maris had hit only 59 homers. He hit number 60 in game number 159, and he hit number 61 on the last day of the season. Babe Ruth still held the record for 154 games. Maris' record of 61 home runs appeared in the book with an asterisk after it. At the bottom of the page there was this note, " *In 162-game season."

The same kind of problem confronted Maury Wills, fleet-footed shortstop of the Los Angeles Dodgers in 1962. Late in the season Wills was approaching Ty Cobb's record of 96 stolen bases in one season, which had been accomplished in 1915. After 154 games Wills had stolen only 95 bases, one less than Cobb's record. But because of the longer season he still had eight games to play.

Baseball Commissioner Ford Frick ruled—as he had done with Roger Maris—that a new record could not be recognized unless it was established over a 154 game schedule. So Wills' record, like Maris', would have an asterisk after it, to denote that it had been set during a 162-game schedule.

But this time Frick was mistaken. Sportswriters and Dodger fans who knew their statistics soon pointed out his error.

In 1915 Cobb had actually used 156 games to set

his record. At the end of 154 games, he had stolen 94 bases. But Cobb's team, the Detroit Tigers, had to replay two games. The Georgia Peach had taken advantage of those games to steal another pair of bases: number 95 in game number 155, and number 96 in game number 156. In 154 games, Wills had stolen 95 bases and was really one base ahead of Cobb. In game number 155 Wills failed to steal a base, so the contest came down to the 156th game. Could Wills tie or break Cobb's record in the same number of games?

More than 20,000 fans watched the deciding game in Busch Stadium, St. Louis. Most of them were rooting for the Cardinals but they also rooted for the Dodger shortstop in his duel with Ty Cobb.

Leading off in the first inning, Wills failed to reach first. But in the third inning he rapped a solid base hit against Cardinal pitcher Larry Jackson. Everyone in the ballpark, including Jackson, knew that Wills would be off for second as soon as he got a good jump. Jackson went into a shortened stretch, watching Wills carefully. Then he delivered a pitch to the plate. Wills shot down the base path to second. Catcher Carl Sawatski fired to second, but the ball arrived too late. Wills had stolen his 96th base and the St. Louis fans roared their appreciation.

In the seventh inning Wills slapped out another base hit. Here was his chance to set a new record.

Maury Wills steals his 97th base.

Larry Jackson tried desperately to prevent the new record. He held Wills close to the bag, then delivered a fastball to the plate, so that catcher Sawatski could get off his throw a split second sooner. Wills was not to be denied. His legs churning, little Maury streaked into second and arrived a heartbeat ahead of Sawatski's perfect throw. Actually, Wills had beaten Cobb's record. The Tiger immortal had stolen 96 bases in 156 games, while Wills had stolen 97 in the same number of games.

The game was stopped, and Wills was presented

with the base itself, to commemorate his record.
Two things marred the celebration. One was that
the Cardinals won the game, 13-2. A second was
that Commissioner Frick refused to change his ruling—Wills had beaten Ty Cobb fair and square,
but the official record book would still show an asterisk next to Maury's record.

Wills continued to steal bases. At the end of the
season the Dodgers and Giants were tied and the
two teams played a three-game playoff for the National League championship. So Wills played in
165 games and stole 104 bases. With or without the
asterisk, Maury Wills has his name in the record
book. And people who know their statistics know
that he was one base faster than the great Ty Cobb.

McGinnity's Nickname

Baseball players earn nicknames for various reasons. Ty Cobb was called "The Georgia Peach" because he was a "peachy" ballplayer and because he came from the state of Georgia, which is known for its peach crops. Robert Rolfe, the old Yankee third baseman, was "Red" because that was the color of his hair. Lou Gehrig became known as "The Iron Horse," because he played over 2,000 games in a row and seemed as tireless and unstoppable as a railroad locomotive or "iron horse."

Joe McGinnity, star pitcher for the New York Giants, earned his nickname because of his fantastic stamina.

It was August 1, 1903. McGinnity, a leading pitcher for the New York Giants, was scheduled to pitch the first game of a doubleheader against the Boston Braves. He felt strong, sure of himself. McGinnity was certain he could beat the Braves—and he did, by a score of 4-1. He allowed the opposition just seven hits.

"Skipper, I'm not tired," McGinnity said to his manager, John McGraw, between games. "Why don't you let me pitch the second game too?"

McGraw eyed the pitcher for a moment. If McGinnity could pitch again, another pitcher could be rested for the next game. "Okay," he said. "If you want to, go ahead and pitch."

The New York hurler did a splendid job in the second game. Only once did he weaken. In the sixth Boston bunched a few of their hits and scored two runs. But McGinnity allowed no more runs, and the Giants went on to win 5-2. He allowed Boston only six hits in the second game.

On August 8th, only a week later, New York tangled with their arch-rivals, Brooklyn, in another doubleheader. Again McGinnity started in the opener and won handily, 6-1, allowing eight hits. Brooklyn scored its lone run in the first inning, but the Giants scored four in their half and won easily.

"I'd like to pitch the second game, Mr. McGraw," McGinnity said to his manager. And once more McGraw agreed.

McGinnity not only pitched well, he scored a run in a strange incident. He got to first, then promptly tried to steal second. He made it safely, but interference was called on the Brooklyn fielder, and McGinnity was awarded third base.

The Brooklyn team was furious over the call. The players clustered around the umpire, complaining bitterly that nobody had interfered with the runner. The Brooklyn pitcher put the ball down on the rubber and went over to join in the argument.

McGraw, who was coaching at third, noticed that nobody had called a time out. The plate was unguarded, the ball was on the mound, and the pitcher was shouting at the umpire. The manager told McGinnity, "Get moving—quick!" McGinnity ran home, scoring a run and gaining credit for another stolen base. The Brooklyn players sheepishly returned to their positions.

As it turned out, McGinnity's run was a big one. Going into the ninth, the Giants trailed 3-2. But they scored two runs and won 4-3. If McGinnity hadn't scored, the Giants might not have won, and McGinnity might not have won his second straight doubleheader.

As August progressed, McGinnity took his regular turn at pitching but didn't have any more two-game performances. Then on August 31st the Giants had a doubleheader against Philadelphia. McGinnity started the opener and took care of the opposition on five hits, winning 4-1. For the third time that month he asked permission to pitch the second game. McGraw again gave him the green light. And this time McGinnity had an easy second game. His teammates clouted the ball all over the field and McGinnity won 9-2.

After that he was no longer Joe. The fans and the newspapers began calling him "Iron Man" McGinnity. He wasn't the only man to pitch both games of a doubleheader, but he had done it three times in one month and won all six games.

When the season ended he led the majors in games pitched with 55, in complete games with 44 and in number of victories with 32. Only an iron man could have accomplished that, even if he pitched only one game at a time.

Unlucky Lou

For most of his major league career, Lou Gehrig played in the shadow of his Yankee teammate, Babe Ruth. No matter what Gehrig did, Ruth did something just a little bit more spectacular.

For example, in 1927, Gehrig's third full season with the Yankees, Lou was a terror at the plate, hitting 47 homers, driving in 175 runs and batting a whopping .373. He should have earned all the headlines in all the New York newspapers. However, that was the same year Babe Ruth hit his record 60 home runs, and all the fans were talking about the Babe.

But at least Gehrig could comfort himself with the knowledge that he was a member of one of baseball's greatest teams. The New York Yankees were always in the thick of a pennant battle.

Once in a while, however, even the Yankees had a bad day. The game against the Washington Senators on April 26, 1931, was one of the worst of all. The Yankees played more like a bad minor league team than the proud champions they were. And as it turned out, Lou Gehrig was the victim of their mistakes.

In the third inning Washington infielder Ossie Bluege sent a blooper over the infield. Yankee right fielder Dusty Cooke raced in to make a shoestring catch, but his spikes caught in the turf. He stumbled and fell hard. The ball rolled away on the outfield grass. First baseman Gehrig chased the ball, but by the time he fired it back to the infield, Bluege had crossed the plate. Undoubtedly, it was the shortest home run on record.

Since the Yankees were short of outfielders due to injuries, pitcher Red Ruffing was sent to right field. But Red wouldn't make any hard throws be-

Lou Gehrig swings and misses during practice.

cause he was afraid he might hurt his arm.

Later in the game, Yankee outfielder Sam Byrd fell down chasing a drive by Joe Cronin. This one went for a three-bagger. Yankee pitchers threw two wild pitches, and a Washington run scored on both of them. Also, during the course of the contest, the Yanks somehow managed to get two runners on the same base.

Gehrig's misfortune came about when he stepped into the batter's box with teammate Lyn Lary on base. The Washington pitcher sent a fastball over the plate, and Gehrig hammered it high and far over the fence. It was automatically a home run—or was it?

For reasons never fully explained, Lary went around second, stepped on third, and then instead of trotting home, he went directly to the Yankee dugout. Gehrig didn't notice what Lary had done and continued jogging around the bases. The umpire promptly ruled Gehrig out because he had passed the runner. Instead of a home run, he received credit for a triple.

Gehrig didn't realize it then, but Lary's boner was to hurt him at the end of the year. For in 1931, both Babe Ruth and Lou Gehrig hit 46 home runs. They finished in a tie for the home run leadership in the American League. If Lyn Lary had crossed the plate in April, Lou Gehrig would have won the home run championship by himself.

The Switchers

Whenever a manager knows that the opposing team will use a righthanded pitcher, he tries to insert as many lefthanded batters as possible. It is a well-known fact that hitters do better against a pitcher of the opposite hand. When a righthanded pitcher throws a curve to a righthanded batter, it spins *away* from the hitter, so that quite often he can't hit the ball solidly with his bat. But the ball would be curving *in* to a lefthanded hitter, and he can pull the ball into a corner for an extra-base hit.

One reason for Mickey Mantle's great success was the fact that he was a "switch hitter." He batted left or right, depending on whether he was facing a southpaw or a righthander. Mickey always batted from the "opposite" side, gaining a slight advantage over any pitcher.

Down in the minor leagues in the 1920s, there was a young shortstop named Paul Richards. Young Richards was one of the very few players in the history of the game who could throw equally well with either hand. When he played shortstop he threw righthanded, because a lefthander would be at a disadvantage at that position. (All major league shortstops for many years have thrown righthanded.)

One day, Richards' manager ran into a difficult problem. A couple of his pitchers were sick, and his others were tired. The manager had simply run out of pitchers! Richards could throw well enough and volunteered to try his luck.

The infielder-turned-pitcher got by the first two batters. The third hitter was a switch hitter. Since Richards was pitching righthanded, the batter stepped into the batter's box hitting lefty.

Richards gazed at the batter thoughtfully for a moment, then took the glove off his left hand and fitted it on his right hand. He went into his windup as a southpaw.

Immediately, the batter called time out. He

walked around the catcher and then took his stance as a righthanded batter.

So Richards put the glove back on his left hand. Once more the batter called time, and again switched, this time back to a lefty position. Not to be outdone, Richards switched too.

Finally the umpire called time out and motioned to both players. "How about it, boys?" he growled. "Are we goin' to keep this up all day?"

"I don't care what he does," said the batter. "I can switch all I like. There's no rule that says I can't."

They might have hopped around the batter's box and the pitcher's rubber forever had not Richards relented. He decided to throw one pitch lefthanded and the next one righthanded no matter where the batter stood.

The count went to three balls and two strikes. And on the next pitch, the batter walked.

One Pitch from the Minors

When a young player comes up to the major leagues, he needs both talent and luck to stay there —especially during his first weeks with the team. One play can sometimes decide whether he will be sent to the minors or stay with the big league club.

One player whose baseball future once hung on one pitch was Yankee pitcher Joe Page. Page was a lefthanded pitcher with a steaming fastball. When he turned it loose, batters were helpless. Joe's fastball had a "jump" to it, making it even harder to hit. But the trouble was that even Page himself didn't know where the ball was going. One day he threw a pitch at the outside corner, knee high. The ball started toward the corner and the catcher was ready for it. But then it suddenly jumped. The batter swung low and missed—just as the pitch sliced up over the plate, belt high. And no one was more surprised than Joe Page!

The husky southpaw first came to the Yankees in 1944, and manager Joe McCarthy thought he had a winner. Page's fastball was as fast as any in the league—or so the batters said. But for the first few years, Page couldn't win consistently. His pitches were almost as wild as they were fast.

"Joe," manager McCarthy would say, "you're one of the fastest pitchers in baseball. Why can't you win?"

The pitcher would shrug hopelessly. "I don't know, skipper," he would mutter.

By 1947, it was sink or swim for Joe Page. The Yankees had a new manager named Bucky Harris. Harris was a slow, easy-going man, quick with the compliments, the pat on the back. Even so, Harris was worried about Page. He was 29 years old and in three years, he had had records of 5-7, 6-3 and 9-8. It was hardly the kind of record a pitcher needed to stay with a club like the Yankees.

One day Harris called Page aside. "Joe," he said bluntly, "I can't keep you if you don't produce.

Maybe you were never meant to be a starting pitcher. From now on you'll be a relief pitcher. Your home is in the bullpen."

Other Yankee pitchers had been trying to help Page. One of these was Bill Bevens, a young righthander. Bevens didn't last long in the majors. He developed a sore arm and retired after the 1947 season. But Bevens knew his business.

"How do you hold the ball for your fast one?" he asked Page one day.

Page gripped the baseball with his two pitching fingers over the seams where they came closest together. "Like this," he said.

Bevens shook his head. "Try it this way," he advised, putting his fingers on the seams where they were widest apart.

Page tried it Bevens' way. He seemed to gain better control.

Meanwhile, Bucky Harris had nearly decided to send Page back to the minors. He just couldn't keep a mediocre pitcher. Too many good young pitchers were waiting for a chance.

On May 26th the turning point came. The Yanks were playing Boston, and the Red Sox were hot at the plate. In the third inning they knocked Frank "Specs" Shea out of the box. They had the bases loaded and nobody out when Joe Page was called in.

The first batter was one of the Red Sox' sluggers,

Rudy York. Gritting his teeth, Page delivered three fast balls. All were wide of the mark. If Page threw one more ball, York would walk, forcing in a run. And Page knew that if he walked the batter, he himself would take a walk back to the minor leagues.

Page took a deep breath and looked around his infield. He turned back to face the batter. The southpaw went into his windup and delivered—a strike. Then he threw a second strike. On the next pitch, York took a big swing, and he missed. Strike three!

The next batter was the dangerous Bobby Doerr. Page reared back and threw nothing but fastballs. Doerr struck out. Shortstop Ed Pellagrini was the next batter. Page got him on an easy fly to the outfield. He was out of the inning!

For the next six innings Joe Page kept pouring in his fast pitch, and the batters swung at empty air. He allowed just two hits and fanned eight batters. How could Bucky Harris send him down to the minors after such a performance? He couldn't. Still, if Page had walked that first batter, he might never have pitched to another major league batter.

That was the turning point for Joe Page. In 1947 he became the best relief pitcher in the American League. He won 14 and lost 8, and saved many more games for the pennant-winning Yanks.

In the World Series that year, Page was abso-

After saving the 1947 World Series for the Yankees, Joe Page celebrates in the locker room.

lutely superb. In the seventh game he pitched five scoreless innings in relief to save both the game and the Series for the Yankees. The man who was a World Series hero in October was the same man who came one pitch from being sent to the minors in May.

Ruth's Last Great Game

When the 1934 season was over, Babe Ruth drew a sigh of relief. It had been his 21st year in the major leagues. He was almost 40 years old. His batting eye had lost its keen edge and his body was stiff and sore. In 1934 he batted only .288 and hit a mere 22 home runs for the New York Yankees. Babe was finished and he knew it. In fact he had already announced his plans to retire.

But Ruth wasn't quite finished with baseball. The Boston Braves were a mediocre team that attracted few paying customers. Their management wanted someone like Ruth to bring people out to the games. In spite of his age, Babe was still a great hero, and many fans would come to the games just for the chance to see him in uniform. The great slugger had begun his major league career in Boston, with the Red Sox. In a way, the people were welcoming him home.

Babe signed a contract that made him a vice president of the team and also assistant manager. A clause in his contract called for him to perform "additional duties," but Babe didn't really know what those duties were until just before the 1935 season. Then he found out. Ruth was to become a part-time player.

Ruth realized that the Braves were using him as an added attraction—"like a monkey in a zoo," he was once heard to mutter. Yet he didn't mind too much, for Babe realized that the Braves needed the money, and that they were paying him a good salary to take a few swings at the plate.

Yet Babe was a proud man. He knew that his skills had deserted him, that now he was just a big fat man who had once known days of glory. True, he drew fine crowds wherever he went, but often the crowds were disappointed because the big slugger failed to get his hits. Ruth hated to disappoint the fans.

Things didn't go well during the early weeks of

Babe Ruth comes into home after hitting his first homer for the Braves in April 1935.

the season. Babe developed a cold and couldn't seem to shake it. His batting average was a lowly .179. And he was more tired than ever. Finally he got so discouraged that he asked for his release. The owner of the Braves, Judge Emil Fuchs, begged Ruth to hang on just a little longer. If Ruth continued to attract crowds, Boston might just manage to pay off its debts. Reluctantly, Ruth agreed.

On May 25th Ruth and the Braves were in Pittsburgh. A good crowd was on hand to see the former superstar in action. A few of the Pittsburgh fans taunted him, saying that he was just a has-been and had no business on a major league diamond. Those close to the Babe saw his lips tighten grimly, his eyes glint dangerously.

There was a man on base when Babe came to bat in the first inning. The pitcher was a righthander named Red Lucas. Ruth lashed his bat around and lofted a home run into the right field stands.

In the third inning when Babe came to bat again, the Pirates had changed pitchers. The veteran Guy Bush was on the hill. Bush was a good, experienced pitcher. The previous year, with the Chicago Cubs, Bush had won 18 games and the year before that he was a 20-game winner.

Ruth was still grim, still angry. Bush delivered, Ruth swung—and the result was another 2-run homer.

When Ruth came to bat again, Pirate manager Pie Traynor decided that Ruth was too tired to hit any more homers. Traynor thought the slugger would manage to pull the ball toward right field, but would probably hit an ordinary fly ball or a simple grounder. Traynor ordered the outfield to shift to the right and play deep. The infield also shifted, so that both the shortstop and second baseman were on the right side of second base. But Ruth crossed up the Pirate strategy. He reached out and poked a single through the wide-open shortstop hole.

In the seventh inning Babe came to bat again. Now, reasoned the Pirate manager, Babe was surely too tired to swing from the heels. How wrong he was! For Babe Ruth unloaded one of the longest home runs ever seen in Pittsburgh.

The fans rose to their feet and cheered the Babe every step of his path around the bases. They did not know then that it was the last home run Babe Ruth was to hit in his glorious career—Number 714.

That game took just about all of Babe Ruth's energy. The next day he struck out three times. A couple of days later, he entered a game as a pinch hitter and walked. He came up once more a few days later and failed again to get a hit.

Tired and aching, Babe asked the Braves to put him on the voluntary retired list. Instead, the Braves released him outright on June 2nd.

The newspapers featured stories of Ruth's final retirement and farewell to baseball. But his real farewell was on May 25th when he showed the fans in Pittsburgh one last glimpse of his greatness.

The Player Who Traded Himself

Baseball players have little to say about being traded. That's up to the club owners. Even if a player is unhappy with a team, he must usually keep playing for it.

Back in 1915, however, one player managed to trade himself. A lefthanded pitcher named Richard "Rube" Marquard was having trouble with his manager, John McGraw. Rube was a good pitcher, but his career had had its ups and downs. After he pitched a no-hitter in the minors, the New York

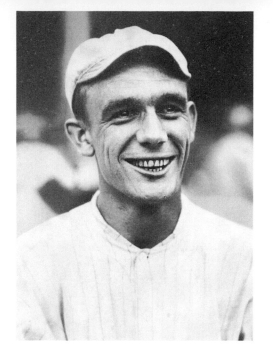

Rube Marquard.

Giants offered him $11,000—a fabulous sum in those days.

Rube didn't do too well during his first couple of seasons, and the fans began calling him "the $11,000 lemon." But then Marquard settled down and won more than twenty games in each of his next three seasons. He became a favorite of the Giants' rooters and was called "the $11,000 beauty."

After those three good years, his fortunes took a turn for the worse. He won only a dozen games in 1914, losing twenty-two. The following year wasn't much better. McGraw was disgusted with the whole team, but he made a particular target of Marquard. Marquard stood it as long as he could, then he decided to have it out with McGraw.

"If I'm such a terrible pitcher, why don't you get rid of me?" Rube demanded.

"Nobody would take you, that's why," McGraw replied.

"Suppose another team did want me," the crafty Marquard said. "How much would the Giants want in return?"

"About $7,500!" snapped McGraw. "That's all you're worth."

Angrily, Marquard asked if he could use the telephone. He called Wilbert Robinson, manager of the Brooklyn team. Robinson had once been connected with the Giants, and had always liked Marquard's pitching. Besides, Marquard had pitched a no-hitter against Brooklyn early in the season.

"Robbie," said Rube when the Brooklyn manager was on the other end of the line, "would you like a good lefthanded pitcher?"

"Sure," replied Robinson immediately. "Who's the pitcher?"

"Me, Rube Marquard. McGraw wants to get rid of me. He says you can have me for $7,500."

Then and there, Marquard was traded to Brooklyn. And the following year Brooklyn won the National League pennant, helped in no small part by Marquard's 14 victories. McGraw, a great manager, had let his temper get the best of him, and he practically handed the pennant to his hated rivals.

Rookie Series

In 1931 the Philadelphia Athletics met the St. Louis Cardinals in the World Series for the second year in a row. In 1930 the Athletics had beaten the Cards in six games. St. Louis wanted to even the score, but that didn't seem likely. The A's had too much power, too much pitching, and one of baseball's great managers, Connie Mack. Still, in a short series anything could happen.

The Cardinals had one new face, a young man named John "Pepper" Martin, who had just finished his first full season with the Cardinals. He had done extremely well, hitting .300. He also amazed fans with his baserunning, using a leaping, head-first slide. Still, the Cards were counting on their veterans to carry the load: "Sunny Jim" Bottomley, the first baseman who had batted .348 during the regular season; Chick Hafey, the slugging outfielder (.349); second baseman Frankie Frisch (.311); and a rookie hurler named Paul Derringer who had scored 18 victories.

In the first game, Martin came to bat in the first inning. The Cardinals had already scored one run and Pepper hit a double that scored another. The Cards went ahead 2-0. Then in the fourth Martin singled but was put out in a double play. He singled again in the sixth. This time he dared fate by trying to steal against the A's great catcher Mickey Cochrane. He slid head-first into second, inches ahead of Cochrane's throw. Pepper fanned in the eighth; but it hadn't been a bad day's work—three hits in four times at bat. Unfortunately, the rest of the Cardinals had not done as well. Philadelphia won 6-2.

In the second game, the Cardinals were led by pitcher Bill Hallahan, who held the Athletics to only three hits. But the Cardinals needed some runs to win. In the second inning, when Pepper came up for the first time, he smacked the ball into the outfield for what looked like a clean single. But

Pepper didn't stop at first and by the time the surprised Athletics recovered, he was standing on second with a double. A few pitches later, he stole third. Finally, he scored on a sacrifice fly.

Pepper grounded out in the fourth, but in the seventh he singled—and stole second. An infield out sent him to third. Then the Cardinals worked a daring play. The batter bunted so that the catcher would have to come out from behind the plate. At the same time, Martin was racing home from third. Martin crossed the plate before Cochrane could field the ball and tag him, scoring the Cardinals' second run. In two games he had chalked up five hits, stolen three bases and scored on a squeeze play against the best catcher in baseball.

The scrappy outfielder continued to harass the Athletics in the third game. He singled in the second inning and doubled in the fourth, scoring two of the Cardinals' five runs. The Cards won 5-2.

In the fourth game the Athletics' pitcher George Earnshaw was untouchable, shutting out the Cards 3-0. Earnshaw allowed only two hits, both of them to Pepper Martin: a single in the fifth (he stole second) and a double in the eighth.

The amazing young rookie had become everybody's favorite. During the fifth game, at Philadelphia, the Athletics fans cheered every time Pepper came to the plate. And he didn't disappoint them.

His first time up, Pepper sent a long drive to the

wall in left-center. The ball was caught, but a runner scored from third after the catch. When he came up in the fourth, the Philadelphia infield was playing back, expecting another hard smash. Pepper tapped a perfect bunt and beat it out for a hit. In the sixth Pepper hit one where nobody could get it—into the bleachers for a two-run homer. And he capped the day with another base hit, driving in yet another run. St. Louis won, 5-1. Pepper had driven in four of the runs. Most important, the Cardinals led in the Series, three games to two.

Philadelphia won the sixth game, but the Cardinals came back to win the Series in the seventh game. This time they won without Martin's help— he went hitless in the last two games. But he did get on base on a walk and steal another base.

In spite of his 2-game "slump," Martin had been amazing. He had 12 hits in 24 at-bats, for a .500 batting average. His hits included one home run, four doubles and seven singles. He batted in five runs, and scored five runs. He had spoiled George Earnshaw's no-hitter and challenged the powerful throwing arm of catcher Mickey Cochrane, stealing five bases. It was the greatest performance by a rookie in World Series history.

Martin was no flash in the pan. He had a long and distinguished career with the Cardinals. But he never surpassed his amazing performance in his rookie World Series.

Pepper Martin slides safely into home against the A's Mickey Cochrane on a squeeze bunt.

The Greatest Minor League Team

When baseball fans talk about the great ballclubs of the past, they mention the same teams time after time. They start with the New York Yankees of 1927 with the famous "Murderer's Row" line-up, which included Babe Ruth and Lou Gehrig. The Philadelphia Athletics of 1930 boasted such Hall of Fame players as Jimmy Foxx, Al Simmons, Mickey Cochrane and Jimmy Dykes. The fabulous St. Louis Cardinals' "Gas House Gang" of 1934 had such stars as Dizzy and Daffy Dean, Frankie

Frisch, Joe Medwick, Pepper Martin and Leo Durocher.

Most of the discussion of great teams is only about the major leagues. But fans who lived in New Jersey in 1937 will put a minor league team among the greatest clubs of all time: the Newark Bears.

In those days, farm teams were much different than they are today. Since there were only sixteen teams in the American and National Leagues, it was much harder for young players to break into the majors. There were fewer major league places, and young players sometimes spent years in the minors waiting for a major league star to retire or be traded. The major leaguers who were "over the hill" often returned to the minor leagues instead of retiring.

The major league club which had the best system of farm teams was the New York Yankees. Somehow it seemed that their stock of outstanding prospects would never be exhausted. The Yankees' most promising players were often sent to Newark, just across the river from New York. And in 1937, the Newark club had a team of major league quality.

At first base was George McQuinn. That year he batted .329 and hit 21 homers. McQuinn played with the St. Louis Browns later, and ended his career with the Yankees.

At second base was Joe "Flash" Gordon, who

batted only .279, but led the Bears in home runs with 26. He later became a Yankee star.

Nolan Richardson, the shortstop, never could hit well enough to stick in the majors, but he was one of the best fielders ever seen in the minor leagues.

At third base was Babe Dahlgren. A good all-round infielder, Dahlgren hit .340 in 1937. Dahlgren later replaced Lou Gehrig in the Yankee lineup when the great first baseman retired because of illness.

In left field was Jimmy Gleeson, a .299 hitter. Gleeson later played with the Cubs and Reds.

"Suitcase Bob" Seeds was in center field. He batted .303, led the team in runs-batted-in with 112, and clubbed 20 homers. Seeds went on to play with the Indians, Red Sox and Yankees.

In right field was a 20-year-old rookie named Charley "King Kong" Keller. A huge powerful man, Keller led the International League that year in batting, with a .351 average. He became one of the most feared batters in the Yankee line-up.

The Bears had two catchers: Buddy Rosar, who hit .322, and Willard Hershberger, a .325 batter. Rosar played with the Yankees, Indians, Athletics and Red Sox. Hershberger became the Cincinnati Reds' catcher.

Pitchers? Atley Donald won 19 games and was sent up to the Yankees late the following season. Joe Beggs won 21 and later pitched for the Yanks

King Kong Keller (left), one of the heroes of the 1937 Newark Bears, chats with Yankee teammate Joe DiMaggio in 1939.

and Reds. Steve Sundra won 15 and graduated to the Yanks, Senators and St. Louis Browns. Vito Tamulis won 18 and went on to hurl for the Yanks, Browns, Dodgers and Phillies.

The Newark Bears won the pennant by 25½ games! It really wasn't much of a race. In the International League playoffs at the end of the season, the Bears got a scare in the first playoff game, against the Syracuse Chiefs. The Chiefs led 1-0 in the ninth inning. The Bears had two out, nobody on, and Joe Gordon at bat.

Gordon hit a home run to tie the game. The next batter, Jimmy Gleeson, hit another homer, to win it, 2-1. After that, Newark had an easy time with the Chiefs. The Bears then faced Baltimore, which was then in the International League. Again, they swept the opposition aside and gained the right to meet the Columbus team of the American Association in the "Little World Series."

Columbus was a Cardinal farm team, and there were many future major leaguers at Columbus too. Among them was Enos "Country" Slaughter, who joined the Cardinals the next season and played for 19 years in the majors.

The first games were played in Newark at Ruppert Stadium. Columbus thrashed the Bears soundly in their first three encounters. The scores were 5-4, 5-4 and 6-3. One more victory and it would be all over. The supposedly invincible Bears would be dealt a crushing blow.

The Bears had suffered few defeats that season and had made the competition seem easy. Now the question was, could they survive three defeats in a row and still come back against all the odds?

The Bears went to Columbus, Ohio, determined to avenge their losses. And in the first game, they bombed the Columbus pitching, winning by 6-0.

Newark manager Oscar Vitt now had a pitching problem. His regular pitchers were tired. But he had a volunteer—"Spud" Chandler. Chandler had been pitching for the Yankees, but developed a sore arm in mid-season. He had been sent to Newark to get back in shape. It was a risk to start a sore-armed pitcher, but Chandler had apparently recovered. He did an outstanding job, hurling another shutout for the Bears. Newark won 1-0.

After that, Columbus felt the full power of the Newark Bears. The Yankee farm team chopped up the Cardinal farm team in the next two games by scores of 10-1 and 10-4. The Bears had come from behind and done the impossible, winning four straight from the high-flying Columbus club.

In 1938 the Newark Bears won the International League pennant again, this time by "only" 18½ games. However, they lost the Little World Series to Kansas City of the American Association, also a Yankee farmclub.

But after that, the Bears fell into a slump. Their players were so good that they were promoted to the majors, and poor Newark had to begin rebuilding once again.

The
Big
Race

During the winter of 1913-1914, John McGraw gathered together a group of major league players and took them on a tour. He had enough players to form two teams, and he called them "Giants" and "White Sox," although not all of them played for those two teams during the regular season. His teams included Tris Speaker, who normally roamed the outfield for the Boston Red Sox, Sam Crawford, who was Detroit Tiger property, and Germany Schaefer, who was then with the Wash-

Hans Lobert.

ington Senators. Another of McGraw's players was a peppy third baseman named John "Hans" Lobert, who played for the Philadelphia Phillies.

Lobert was a good hitter, having batted .300 or better for four seasons. But he was best known for his speed on the base paths. Before he reached the majors, Lobert spent a season at Johnstown, where he stole 57 bases. Once, at Cincinnati, he circled the bases in $13\frac{4}{5}$ seconds, which was considered extremely fast, and would be judged good time even today.

One day the touring teams stopped at Oxnard, California, to play an exhibition game. The event aroused great interest, and the wooden stands of the tiny ballpark were filled to capacity. There were also many fans in the outfield, some of them local cowboys mounted on horses.

Before the game Lobert was approached by the mayor of the town. "Mr. Lobert," said the mayor, "we have heard that you are very fast. Would you care to engage in a race?"

"Who's the other runner?" asked Lobert.

"I was thinking of a different kind of race," said the mayor. "How about racing a horse around the bases?"

Lobert refused—at least in the beginning. Finally, McGraw persuaded him to go through with the race. The manager pointed out that many people would be disappointed if he refused, especially the cowboys. Lobert agreed to run the race after the game was over.

However, when news of the race spread, few fans wanted to wait for the game to finish. Many of the spectators placed bets on the outcome. When the seventh inning arrived, the fans would wait no longer.

The "opponent" trotted onto the field. It was a beautiful black cow pony, very fast and agile, capable of making sharp turns. Lobert, the horse and the rider—a Mexican cowboy—walked around the base paths so that the horse would know what it was supposed to do. As they paced around the bases, a newsreel camera followed them, taking silent movies of the scene.

It was agreed that Lobert would circle the bases on the inside of the path, while the horse took the outside. Soon everything was ready. Umpire Bill Klem was appointed referee. A pistol shot was fired—they were off and running!

Lobert got the jump on the horse and led all the way to first. He tagged the bag on the inside, cut sharply and headed for second while the cowpony turned left in a tight circle. Picking up speed, Lobert increased his lead around second base. But now the horse wasn't turning as widely, and as Lobert headed for third, the horse began to crowd him. Lobert was forced to break stride. The crowd cheered wildly for their favorites. Between third and home the horse overtook and passed the runner, just beating him over the plate by a nose.

The horse had won but the issue was not completely settled. For years afterward, Lobert insisted the horse should have been disqualified for crowding him. The horse, he said, had broken the rules of the race.

The Wrong-Way Runner

Many pitchers are terrible hitters. Only a few ever achieve respectable batting averages. One good example was Lefty Gomez, a great pitcher for the New York Yankees. In 14 years he never hit over .200 and he averaged fewer than ten hits a season.

Gomez was such a poor batter that when he did manage to get a hit, sometimes he hardly knew what to do about it. One day he swung at a pitch with all his strength. By accident or good luck he hit the ball solidly, and it flew out along the right-field line, hitting the fence 340 feet away. Lefty was so amazed that he stood near the plate, watching the flight of the ball with fascination. Finally he trotted to first, arriving just as the ball was thrown back to the infield. It was one of the longest singles on record.

Perhaps the poorest-hitting pitcher in the majors was a 19-year-old lefthander named Jimmy St. Vrain, who played with the Chicago Cubs. He pitched twelve games for the Cubs in 1902. But in that brief time he did something that was the talk of baseball for a long time.

Not only did Jimmy fail to get hits, he also had trouble popping a foul or grounding out. Usually, he swung and missed the ball completely.

Perhaps one reason Jimmy always missed the ball was that he didn't concentrate on the pitch. He was a righthanded batter, so he faced first base. Between pitches, he would sneak longing looks at first. How he wished he could get there! It was only ninety feet away, but it might just as well have been a hundred miles. It seemed that the only chance he had to get there was to face a pitcher wild enough to walk him.

One day as he returned sadly to the bench after striking out, Cub manager Frank Selee tapped him on the shoulder. "Jimmy," he said, "you throw left-handed, but you bat righthanded. How come?"

St. Vrain shrugged. "I've always played that way," he said.

"You're a natural lefthander. Why don't you bat lefthanded too? You can't do any worse."

St. Vrain decided to give it a try. On his next trip to the plate he stepped into the lefthanded side of the batter's box and faced the pitcher hopefully.

Jimmy found a pitch he liked and swung. Maybe the manager had been right to change him to a left-handed hitter or maybe Jimmy was just lucky for a change. But he hit the ball and it bounded out toward Honus Wagner at shortstop. It didn't look like a base hit, but Jimmy had at least put the ball in play. It was a big moment for him.

Jimmy dropped his bat and took off like a shot—*toward third base!*

Wagner fielded the ball cleanly, straightened up, and stopped. Why was the batter running toward third? Should he throw the ball to the third base-man and let him make the tag? Wagner finally shook the cobwebs out of his head and tossed the ball to first base. Of course St. Vrain was out—by 180 feet.

Later in the season, Jimmy St. Vrain actually got a few hits. He finished the season with a batting average of .097. As a pitcher, he had won four games and lost six. Where he went after he left the Cubs the record books don't tell us. But long after he was gone he was remembered as the wrong-way runner.

The Rally

The 1929 World Series started out with a surprise. The Philadelphia Athletics were meeting the Chicago Cubs and the A's manager, Connie Mack, was expected to start his pitching ace, Lefty Grove. Instead, the wily old manager had Howard Ehmke start the first game. Ehmke had pitched only 55 innings all season. He was 35 years old and his career seemed finished. But he pitched superbly against the Cubs, striking out 13 batters and winning the first game 3-1.

Manager Connie Mack of the A's poses with catcher Mickey Cochrane (left) and pitcher Lefty Grove.

But there was yet another highlight, at least as strange and exciting as Ehmke's performance. The Athletics won the second game but lost the third. Going into the fourth game, they were hoping to break the Cubs' spirit by gaining their third win. But as the game progressed, the A's hopes seemed to evaporate.

Charlie Root was on the mound for the Cubs, and he was breezing through the Philadelphia line-up with great ease. Meanwhile, Chicago had teed off on Philadelphia's pitchers, scoring a pair of runs in the fourth inning, five runs in the sixth and another in the seventh. Leading by 8-0, the Cubs seemed to have broken the A's spirit.

Philadelphia was always a dangerous team at the plate. Connie Mack's roster was loaded with great hitters. Outfielder Al Simmons had batted a hot .365 during the regular season, first baseman Jimmy Foxx had batted .354 and catcher Mickey Cochrane had hit .331. Other dangerous batters included Jimmy Dykes, the .327-hitting infielder and "Mule" Haas, whose average stood at .313. Al Simmons had batted in 157 runs and hit 34 homers. But even this mighty team would have trouble overcoming an 8-run deficit.

When the A's came up in the bottom of the seventh, Al Simmons led off with a long home run. Jimmy Foxx followed with a single, and "Bing" Miller, the third member of the Philadelphia outfield (he had batted .335 that year) also hit safely. Jimmy Dykes and shortstop Joe Boley also chipped in with singles. Three runs had scored and two men were on base when pinch-hitter George Burns popped up for the first out.

The halt was only temporary. Second baseman Max Bishop came up and hit a single, driving in the fourth run. Suddenly the Athletics were only four runs behind; there were two men on base and only one out. Cub pitcher Charlie Root was taken out for lefthander Art Nehf. It seemed like a good move, for the next batter was lefthanded batter Mule Haas, and lefty pitchers have the edge on lefty batters.

Haas hit a drive to center field which seemed sure to be the second out of the inning. But Cub outfielder Hack Wilson lost the ball in the sun. It rolled all the way to the wall, and by the time it was retrieved, Haas had circled the bases with an inside-the-park home run, scoring behind the two base runners. It was now 8-7.

When Nehf walked Mickey Cochrane, the Cubs changed pitchers again, bringing in relief pitcher "Sheriff" Blake. But the Sheriff couldn't arrest the rally either. Simmons, up for the second time in the inning, singled. Then Foxx singled (his second in the inning), driving in the tying run. The Sheriff was sent to the showers and the fourth Cub pitcher, Pat Malone, entered the fray.

Bing Miller greeted him with a single to load the bases. Jimmy Dykes followed with a double, scoring a pair of runs, giving the A's a 10-8 lead. Joe Boley and pinch-hitter George Burns went out to end the inning, but the A's had scored 10 runs in one inning, the mightiest rally in Series history.

The rest of the game was not very eventful. Connie Mack called on Lefty Grove, his best pitcher, to protect the A's hard-earned lead. The game ended with the score still 10-8.

That 10-run rally broke Chicago's spirit. The Athletics had increased their edge to three games to one and needed only one more game to win the Series.

In the fifth game Connie Mack called on Howard Ehmke again, hoping that the old-timer could work another miracle. But the Cubs knocked him out of the box. When the A's came up in the bottom of the ninth, Chicago was leading 2-0. The Cub pitcher, Pat Malone, retired the first batter but then disaster struck the Cubs again. Max Bishop singled and Mule Haas hit his second homer in two days to tie the score. Then Al Simmons went to work again, booming a long double into the outfield. Dangerous Jimmy Foxx was walked intentionally, but nothing could stop the Athletics. The next batter, Bing Miller, slammed a double that scored the winning run.

The Series was over and the A's had won— thanks to Howard Ehmke, ten runs in one inning and a final "mini-rally" with one out in the ninth.

The Game That Was Won Twice

Basically, baseball is a simple game. The team scoring the most runs after nine—or more—innings is the winner. But sometimes it isn't easy to decide whether or not a run has scored. One of the strangest problems of this kind occurred in the minor leagues, and it took the president of that league to force a decision on both teams.

The Texarkana team of the Texas League was playing Sherman. Texarkana was up in the bottom of the ninth. The score was tied and Texarkana had a man on third with two out.

The Sherman pitcher got two strikes on the next batter. Then, as he wound up for his next delivery, the runner on third took off, trying to steal home. Both umpires were instantly on the alert, watching the runner. The catcher caught the ball and dived for the tag as the runner slid in.

"Safe!" cried the umpire behind the plate. That should have been the winning run for Texarkana. But the manager of the Sherman team had other ideas. He came charging off the bench and confronted the umpire.

"Was that last pitch a ball or a strike?" he demanded.

The umpire was temporarily confused. "What difference does it make?"

"If it was a strike," the manager replied, "then the batter is out and the run doesn't count, because he was struck out before the runner crossed the plate. Now, what's your call, ball or strike?"

The plate umpire shrugged. "To tell you the truth, I don't really know," he admitted. "I was so busy watching the runner, I didn't pay attention to the pitch. Let's ask the other umpire."

But the second umpire didn't know either, for he too had been watching the base runner.

It happened that the president of the league was present, and both managers and the two umpires appealed to him for a decision. The president really didn't know if the pitch was a ball or a strike either, because like everyone else, he had been watching the runner. Still, he had to reach a verdict sooner or later.

"The run doesn't count," said the league president.

Naturally, the Texarkana manager was angry. Even the plate umpire was displeased with the decision. However, the ruling had been given. The official decreed that the game had to be resumed the following day, starting with the tenth inning.

The next day, Sherman led off the top of the tenth with a pair of runs. But in the bottom of the inning Texarkana loaded the bases. The next batter hit a grand-slam home run and Texarkana was declared the winner.

The Texarkana manager, still angry about the call, complained that it was the only game he could remember that his team had to win twice. Still, that was better than winning it once and then losing it.

Too Much Hustle

In 1939 the Brooklyn Dodgers signed a young ball-player who gave promise of becoming one of the greatest stars in the game. He could run like a deer, hit with power and throw a baseball as if a cannon were hidden in his sleeve. On the field he was sure-handed, seldom making an error, regardless of whether he played in the infield or outfield. His name was Harold Reiser, but everyone called him "Pistol Pete."

Above all his skills, the thing that stood out

about Pistol Pete was his hustle. He never quit chasing a fly ball, whether it was catchable or not. And if something got in his way—such as a brick wall—that was just too bad. He would run right through the wall to make the catch—or at least he would try.

When Pistol Pete came to spring training camp in 1939, manager Leo Durocher told him to play shortstop. Pete gobbled up everything hit his way. And as a batter he was a terror. In his first twelve times at bat in exhibition games he collected three home runs, five singles, and four walks—a perfect record!

Yankee manager Joe McCarthy watched Reiser hit a home run off his ace southpaw, Lefty Gomez, and determined to acquire the young man at any cost. The Yanks made an offer for Reiser: $100,000 plus five players. The Dodgers laughed and told the Yankees he wasn't for sale or trade, not at *any* price.

Reiser was barely 20 years old and the Dodgers sent him to the minors for more experience. Reiser took the demotion with good grace, even though he thought he was good enough to play in the majors. In Elmira, he continued to give every play his best effort. He hustled with every ball hit his way and put extra steam with every throw he made. He began to pay the penalty almost immediately.

One day he made a hard throw and felt a sharp

twinge in his right arm. He tried to shake off the pain but couldn't. A few days later the arm was x-rayed. Reiser had broken his arm on the throw.

Pistol Pete never could stand idleness. A month later he was back in action—throwing lefthanded. He played ten games before the horrified Dodger management found out and made him stop. However, Reiser continued to practice throwing left-handed, and in a short time found that he could throw pretty well that way.

In 1940 Reiser appeared in 58 games for the Dodgers. Then in 1941 he was with the Dodgers to stay. No player ever hustled harder than Pistol Pete. He crowded the plate when he batted, almost daring opposing pitchers to bean him. And they did. The first time, he was hit on the head by a pitcher named Ike Pearson. Reiser woke up in the hospital—and resolved not to remain there very long. The next day he had talked the medical staff into discharging him, and he went directly to the ballpark where he suited up.

Reiser sat nervously on the bench while the Dodgers played to a 7-7 tie. The Dodger pitcher was due up, and on the mound was the same relief pitcher who had beaned him, Ike Pearson. Reiser begged manager Leo Durocher to send him in as a pinch-hitter and Durocher agreed.

Reiser hit a home run.

Two weeks later, while chasing a fly ball, Reiser

crashed into the wall and was knocked out. In August of that year he was beaned again.

Somehow despite his injuries, Pistol Pete Reiser hung in there. He finished the season with a .343 average, winning the National League batting title. He was the first rookie ever to win it.

In 1942 Reiser continued to terrorize opposing pitchers. They were afraid to throw the ball anywhere near the plate when he was at bat. By July he was hitting .381. Then in a game at St. Louis, Reiser put some extra hustle into chasing a fly ball —and he crashed into the wall again.

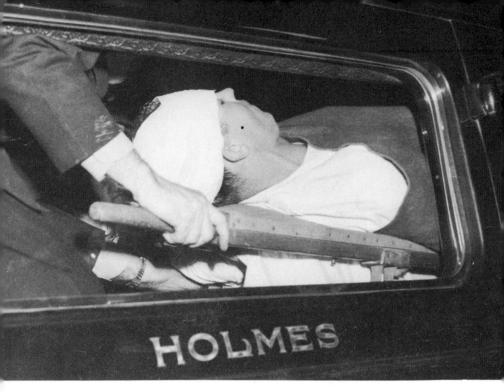

Showing his daredevil spirit, Reiser slides into home (left). Above, he is taken to the hospital after running into an outfield wall.

The doctor examined the hustling youngster and advised him to give up baseball for the rest of the season. But Reiser didn't agree. Two days later he had talked his way out of the hospital again. He went to the ballpark and suited up. Once again he was sent in to pinch-hit. As usual, Reiser delivered the hit that won the game. It should have been an extra base blow, but Reiser collapsed rounding first base. When he awoke, he was in the hospital again.

Somehow, Pistol Pete got through the season. He batted .310.

After the 1942 season Reiser entered the Army

(the United States was fighting in World War II). On his Army unit team Pistol Pete was up to his old tricks. While chasing a fly ball, he cracked through a temporary wooden fence, knocking himself out.

When Pete returned to Brooklyn after the war, the Dodgers tried everything to keep their young star in one piece. The team even put padding on the walls. It didn't help. In 1947 he crashed into a wall so hard that it was necessary to perform an operation to remove a blood clot in his head.

No amount of pleading could make him take it easier. Pete Reiser knew how to play baseball only one way—all-out hustle. Finally the Dodgers gave up on him. He was traded to Boston, and from there he went to Pittsburgh. After a few games with Cleveland in 1952, he was finished in the majors.

During his career, Pistol Pete Reiser was carried off the field no less than eleven times. One way or another, he suffered two broken ankles, torn cartilage in his left knee, a broken bone in his right elbow, ripped muscles in his left leg, and a wide assortment of concussions, contusions and abrasions.

Many baseball fans still insist that Harold Reiser could have been one of the finest ballplayers in the National League, for he certainly had all the talent. But he had too much of one important quality— too much hustle.

I Can
Do It
Myself

Al Schacht was one of the funniest men ever to play baseball. Most of the time his zany stunts worked, and the spectators would roar with laughter. When his tricks backfired, they were even funnier.

In 1928 a memorial game was played in honor of Eddie Plank, a Hall of Fame pitcher. The two teams were composed of pick-up sides. Coaches, minor leaguers and amateurs played alongside the big leaguers. Nobody cared which side won—the game was all in fun.

Schacht, who was the perfect player for such a game, was chosen to pitch for one of the teams. He loudly announced that he was going to retire the side in one-two-three order.

Schacht did manage to get the first two men out. The third batter was Ike Powers, a batting practice pitcher. Ike seldom had a bat in his hands, so naturally he was a very poor hitter.

Al Schacht with his famous giant glove.

As Powers stepped into the batter's box, Schacht pretended to double over with laughter. He pointed to Powers derisively and snapped his fingers as if to say, "You're as good as finished." Then he called in all his outfielders and infielders. He told them to head for the dugout. Only Schacht and the catcher were left on the field.

Schacht bowed grandly to the crowd, then wound up and delivered a pitch to the plate. It was a slow ball, belt high, right over the middle. Powers swung with all his might and connected. Away flew the ball into the outfield.

But nobody was out there to catch the drive. Schacht turned and ran, chasing the ball all the way to the fence. Powers was out of breath by the time he had reached second base, and his sprint around the bases was more like the gallop of a tired horse. Schacht reached the ball, picked it up and threw toward home.

The ball bounced near the infield and rolled toward the plate where the catcher was waiting. At last the ball arrived. So did Ike Powers. The catcher reached for the ball and tagged the runner.

"You're out!" called the umpire when he stopped laughing.

Al Schacht walked back to the bench, huffing and puffing. "You see," he said triumphantly when he caught his breath. "I told you I could do it myself."

Index